Flaps and Chats

Flaps and Chats

My own personal journal of bereavement and grief

BY

HELEN CONEYWORTH-SMITH

The Choir Press

Copyright © 2023 Helen Coneyworth-Smith

All rights reserved. No part of this publication may be reproduced or transmitted in any form or by any means, electronic or mechanical including photocopying, recording or any information storage or retrieval system, without prior permission in writing from the publishers.

The right of Helen Coneyworth-Smith to be identified as the author of this work has been asserted by him in accordance with the Copyright, Designs and Patents Act 1988

First published in the United Kingdom in 2023 by

The Choir Press

ISBN 978-1-78963-414-3

Acknowledgements

To all my dear close friends.

Thank you for laughing and crying with me, hugging me, and always giving me your unconditional love.

Also, for never judging me, even in my wildest, craziest times.

A big thank-you to Debbie Wilkinson Photography in Hull, for the photograph on the front cover of the book and for making me look glamorous again.

Dedication

To my beloved husband, Andrew.
The person who believed in me,
supported me and showed me true love.
'I hide my tears when I say your name,
but the pain in my heart is still the same'.
Until we meet again.
Love always from your Lizzie
XXXXX

Never regret anything that has happened in your life.
It cannot be changed, undone or forgotten.
So, take it as a lesson, and move on.
Anon

PART ONE
2021

CHAPTER 1   – SUMMERTIME SADNESS 1

CHAPTER 2   – BORN TO DIE 4

CHAPTER 3   – BUILD A BRIDGE AND GET OVER IT 8

CHAPTER 4   – CHATLINES AND BLURRED LINES 12

CHAPTER 5   – SEX CHATS AND FANNY FLAPS 16

CHAPTER 6   – LET ME BE YOUR FANTASY 25

CHAPTER 7   – LITTLE LIES 29

CHAPTER 8   – ONE-NIGHT STAND 32

CHAPTER 9   – BOTOX AND BLOW JOBS 36

CHAPTER 10 – SAVE A PRAYER 43

CHAPTER 11 – DRINKING FROM THE BOTTLE 48

CHAPTER 12 – OH CUM, ALL YE UNFAITHFUL 52

CHAPTER 1

SUMMERTIME SADNESS

'I have one massive regret in my life – that I was still working HERE when my husband was fucking dying.'

Those words are what I almost spat out to my ex-employer at my exit interview. It was said with hatred, spite and venom, and I meant it. Every bloody word of it. I even shocked myself by saying it with such ferocity.

I was fucking done with it all. Pathetic working policies, meaningless statistics, absurd appraisals, ridiculous verbal warnings – I was done with it all! Bloody big time!

Let's rewind eighteen months to the beginning of the story. Eighteen months that have changed my life – forever.

*

COVID was unfortunately a direct, and indirect, killer for some people. Before the pandemic, Andrew, my husband, had been having regular tests and check-ups at hospital. He had many illnesses and disabilities; the main one now being monitored was idiopathic pulmonary fibrosis, known as IPF, part of COPD. An incurable lung disease, causing breathing difficulties and a shortened lifespan. He had to go for regular oxygen level check-ups and lung flow checks.

During COVID, these check-ups suddenly stopped. The specialist nurses, who were excellent, did telephone consultations instead. Andrew was isolating and so was I, scared in case either of us caught COVID, as he was in the high risk category. I was working from home, which took the pressure off me and gave me slightly more time with Andrew as it saved travelling time each day.

The night Andrew died was, and still is, a shock. He collapsed and died right in front of me. *Obviously*, I did CPR. *Obviously*, I rang the emergency services at the same time. *Obviously*, I tried to resuscitate him in any way I could. Even shouting his name loudly, so much so that I could hardly breathe, then shouting and swearing to the emergency services to 'just FUCKING hurry up!' Then I found myself apologising for my rudeness. It wasn't their fault; they were trying to help. I was in a hot sweat from the effort of continual CRP. I remember taking off my sweatshirt as I thought I was going to pass out from the momentum of the continual chest compressions, which were getting stronger and more rapid the longer I did them. I certainly wasn't moving from where I was knelt on the bedroom floor next to him, to open the window to let some cool air into the room. I was almost breathless with trying not to cry and knowing in my mind that I COULDN'T cry – not yet. I had to go on autopilot and turn off any emotion – to bloody save him. This was fucking life and death, and I knew it.

I could feel a lump rising in my throat and tried to swallow it. My mouth was dry, but I knew I had to carry on regardless. The emergency services on the phone were on loudspeaker and telling me repeatedly to S-L-O-W DOWN. I was going too fast; they were counting slowly and calmly to me, for me to follow their lead. I knew I was going too fast and too hard, but I was fucking bloody desperate and panicking. Wouldn't anyone be in my situation?

'No,' I snapped back. 'I CAN'T get to a defibrillator. It's too far away at the school,' and 'no, I have no one else in the house to help me. I AM ALL ALONE!' Nothing could have prepared me for this. The wait for the emergency services to get to the house seemed to be taking forever. Deep down, I knew it was too late, and I was bloody right.

Andrew's favourite saying to me was 'Helen, you're always right, never wrong. Even when you are wrong, you think you are right!' and we used to laugh. Well, unfortunately, I WAS right this time. He had gone. I would have given my life to be wrong and admit it – just this once.

That whole night will haunt me for the rest of my life, but not as much as the guilt I now had to live with, that I couldn't resuscitate him. He relied on me as his wife and carer; he trusted me to make everything all right and look after him. Now look at the situation. I had let him, and myself, down – bloody big time. I blamed myself as I had always tried to be a good wife in our marriage, 'in sickness and in health' and all that. Well, I couldn't have been that bloody good.

I sat on Andrew's side of the bed and faced the wardrobes, now wishing, respectfully, that everyone would leave me in peace – the paramedics, the police, and whoever else had miraculously just appeared in our bedroom. OUR marital bedroom, private to only us two, not the random people that were now there. They were now asking me questions such as 'Have you any family you can contact?', 'Do you want someone with you?' The answer was 'no' to every question they asked. This now seemed to be one long repetitive question and answer night. I WASN'T ON A FUCKING QUIZ SHOW! I needed to mentally comprehend what I had just witnessed and needed to be left alone without having to talk. I certainly wasn't in the mood for answering any questions.

I laid in bed later that night, still dressed and with all the bedroom lights on. Frightened and alone. I daren't even turn the lights off, and I certainly daren't go to sleep. How the hell would I tell Sheila, Andrew's mother, this news? He was her only child and she doted on him. I knew I would have to tell her in person.

By 8am the next day, I was ready to drive to Sheila's flat in Beverley, to tell her the news that her only son had died. This was going to be yet another traumatic and harrowing day.

CHAPTER 2

BORN TO DIE

It was July 2021, one month after Andrew's funeral. I was still in shock and felt numb. People were now getting the brunt of my anger and I didn't care, when really I should have. Andrew had been in pain for years with complex regional pain syndrome (CRPS), but he didn't know how much pain I was in too. After all, it wasn't a competition. I hid my own illnesses and pains as I had to look after him. I had to be the strong one; I was his carer as well as working, and it was bloody hard. No one else was going to do it. Over the last few years, I had progressively turned into his carer, wife, lover and then almost his mother. I was absolutely shattered but I could hardly blame Andrew. Things had changed, but our love hadn't.

I had suffered severe stomach pains for over five years. I had been to the doctor to tell her about the pains, saying it felt like endometriosis, that I had twenty years' previous. But this pain felt worse, and it was affecting my bowel and stomach and making me vomit and pass out. I have a very good pain threshold and can cope with most pain. The doctor didn't seem unduly bothered, in my opinion, eventually sending me for an ultrasound scan at the local hospital. I pointed and showed them the area that was hurting, all across my fallopian tube region but especially to the right side. The sonographer was a young male and didn't seem to have a clue about the female body. I sighed to myself with exasperation as he said there was a bit of calcified tissue in my fallopian tubes but nothing to worry about. But I still had a mixture of relief and worry with a niggling feeling. Something wasn't quite right.

I left the hospital upset and dejected as no one had listened to my concerns. The instruction, or half-hearted advice, I received from the doctor's receptionist was that if I was in so much pain just to call an ambulance or go to Accident and Emergency at Hull Royal Infirmary.

Then they would diagnose me. I knew I could never do this as I had to look after Andrew; I couldn't leave him on his own. How could I leave him alone in the house? Unable to cook or feed himself, he had to be spoon-fed as he couldn't hold a knife and fork, or even lift a spoon to his mouth.

I was his lifeline, the one who cooked and fed him, the one who wiped his arse and gave him his twenty plus tablets morning and night, having to put each tablet into his mouth individually, trying to put a beaker to his lips for him to take a sip of water for the tablets to go down. The one who dressed and undressed him, the one who washed him and had to attempt to shave him. That was only a fraction of the routine I had to do every single day.

My whole day at work was then spent worrying in case he happened to accidently trip or fall over, as he wouldn't be able to get off the floor. I lived in a constant state of stress and high anxiety. I had no time to myself, but I carried on because I loved him, and he would have done the same for me if the roles had been reversed. I wasn't a quitter; I was strong. I HAD to be strong. Those that have carer's duties will understand.

I plodded on, still in pain, but regularly took some of Andrew's prescription medication to ease it. After all, the medical profession didn't seem to believe me, and prescribed me nothing. The doctor had even put the phone down on Andrew a few months before he passed away. He didn't believe he was even that ill with IPF and refused to help or sign his PIP disability form. Well, here we were, a few months after that telephone conversation, he was now dead. Obviously, he wasn't faking his illnesses then! Ironically, wrongly or rightly – I'm seriously past caring – Andrew had recorded that telephone conversation. I found it and listened to it after his death. It was heartbreaking, as the doctor was so rude, arrogant and disbelieving of him. After that, neither of us had faith in the NHS anymore.

Andrew's controlled medicines, such as tramadol, were excellent for masking my pain, mixing a few diazepam and amitriptyline tablets with it, and I was okay for a while. High as a blooming kite possibly, but the pain was a bit more manageable. We were both sharing controlled drugs to ease our various pains. I was now walking stooped and had to hold onto the right side of my abdomen; otherwise, I would be crying out in pain from the stomach cramps, then would get hot sweats and nausea, but, yeah, it was more manageable. Thank goodness for tablets, any mixture of prescription tablets, I took anything. I was past caring – after all, no one else seemed to care.

I still went to work. I had to. Otherwise, I would only get a verbal and then written warning about my accumulation of points from my absences on the bloody 'Bradford Factor' scale, an unplanned absence benchmark at work. What a load of Human Resources policy bollocks that was. I had only been to Bradford twice in my life. What the heck was the 'Bradford Factor' all about? I wouldn't be going there again. However, my absences would cause Andrew to worry about me losing my job. I was trapped.

Suddenly everyone became bloody medical experts. 'It will be the menopause' ... 'it's gallstones' ... 'it could be IBS or Crohn's,' work colleagues said. 'I have that.' I knew it was none of these; the cramps were like contractions or spasms, as if I was going to give birth but without epidural or any gas and air. How women have a natural birth without pain relief is beyond me; they deserve a medal. At least if I had given birth, the pain would be over with. It wasn't. I was now fed up with throwing up because of the pain and then passing out in the bathroom. But still I continued. Andrew needed me more than ever and I wouldn't, and couldn't, let him down.

Unfortunately, months later, Andrew had gone, so now was the time for me to get a second opinion. This time privately, through work's private healthcare scheme. I made an appointment and went to Spire Hospital. They referred me to a colorectal consultant. As originally thought, it was my bowel, and having a family history of bowel cancer, they needed to check this first. The consultant felt my stomach and asked if I wanted to use the toilet. I said no, I had just been. I immediately felt uneasy and felt he was trying to keep a poker face. I was good at that act too, as I had mastered it to perfection. He then sent me straight away for a scan. He wanted me to come back for the results. I said I would prefer, if possible, a phone call, as the hospital was some 40 miles away.

I knew it was bad news when the consultant rang me at 9.45pm on a Wednesday night, after finishing his private clinic for the day in Leeds – it's funny how you don't forget some things. The tone of his voice said it all, and I knew it wasn't good news. He was making polite conversation and pleasantries. Then he said, 'Mrs Coneyworth, you have a large mass – it must come out immediately. It's too big for keyhole surgery. It's probably a liposarcoma that's been growing for quite a while. From the scan, it looks like it may have latched onto your bowel, bladder, stomach or other organs. This is very serious. We do not have time for a biopsy. Let me arrange for another test, and scans, and we will discuss things then. I will ask my secretary to book you an appointment. She will call you with a date for surgery.' I nearly dropped my phone with shock.

I googled the word liposarcoma as I hadn't a clue what it meant. I could hardly spell it, never mind pronounce it. I wished I hadn't. It meant cancer. I looked at the life expectancy. I wished I hadn't. I suddenly felt an overwhelming sense of doom and wondered if this was how Andrew felt in his final few days. God, I needed him so much; for him to hold me, hug me and tell me everything would be okay. Even though I knew it would be a lie, I just needed him, and even a little white lie didn't matter, just to make me stay here. Otherwise, what was the bloody point of it all? The truth was that there actually wasn't any point anymore.

CHAPTER 3

BUILD A BRIDGE AND GET OVER IT

The Humber Bridge is an icon to me for so many reasons. I'm intrigued with its structural engineering and construction, and the clean straight lines will always fascinate me. Possibly my OCD kicking in, but I don't care. It's a truly remarkable bridge that no other bridge in the world can compete with, in my eyes. To many people, it is a sign that 'we are nearly home' when coming back from holidays. Now the bridge had another fascination for me: the height of the walkway and the depth of the water below. My brother used to help with Humber Rescue and had told me about the bridge jumpers, some stuck in the mud when they jumped, broken bones from the impact of the water, some people were never found – washed out into the North Sea. He used to tell me it would be a horrible death to jump from the bridge. But what did he care? We weren't speaking and he didn't even know about Andrew passing or my recently diagnosed tumour.

I had to have a good long think about whether I had a future, ANY future, before doing anything hasty. I knew all paperwork such as my will was sorted. I frantically took it out of the filing cabinet in my office at home and read it, repeatedly. What would Andrew say if he could see the state of me at that precise time? Crying non-stop, thinking the unthinkable. His death was a terrible tragedy. Did I want mine to be like that too? I put the will back into its folder and slammed the metal filing cabinet drawer shut. I had to get a bloody grip before I did something seriously stupid. I went to bed sobbing, uncertain of any future I had. How could I give up everything we had both worked so hard for? What was worse? Committing suicide, dying on the operating table, or living with the aftermath of the tumour and cancer? I knew the ultimate outcome for any of these was the same – it was death.

A few weeks later, I invited Garry back into my life. I had unfinished business that needed finishing if I was going to do something drastic. Garry was my first proper boyfriend when I was seventeen years old, the person I lost my virginity to. We were together for nearly two years. I found his name on Facebook and made contact, reminding him of who I was, just in case he had forgotten. He had probably put his bad memories of me out of his mind, and I wouldn't have blamed him. He accepted my friend request. We sent a few messages to each other, just polite chit-chat reminiscing about the past in Hessle and our drinking days at the Lincoln Castle on the Foreshore. This time, I sent him the message I was dreading. I hadn't time for delaying things; it would only make me edgy again and God knows what I might have done. I just wrote a message to the point – *Garr, I* **need** *to see you. I have had some news that I have to have an operation and seriously do not think I am going to survive it. I need to see you to say goodbye.*

He rang me straight away. 'Helen, I will come and see you, but to say hello not goodbye.' Blooming Garry, he was always thinking calmly and logically, just like the Garry I used to go out with forty years ago.

I was sobbing down the phone to him without even taking a breath. 'Garr, I have to have an operation. I might have cancer and there's something wrong with my bowel. They are going to remove some of it and I might have to have a colostomy bag for a few months – or forever!'

Garry tried to calm me down; he probably thought I was deranged and he had a lucky escape from marrying me when we were both young. I was almost having a nervous breakdown but knew I could still trust him. We had history. I wanted us to still be friends. He now had to be the one who grounded me, who had to make me see sense, to stop me doing anything irrational.

He had been my foundation, my rock when I was seventeen years old, making me realise that my family WERE cruel and unloving. He was the first person ever to show me love and affection. But then my mother had knowingly destroyed our love, and our relationship, by banning him from the house, HER HOUSE. When I did sneak out of the house to see Garry, she would guess and put the house key in the front door keyhole, so I couldn't get my key in from the outside and turn it to unlock it. She was evil and spiteful. However much I knocked and banged on the door with my fists, she wouldn't let me in. By midnight, I had usually given up shouting and knocking at the door and resigned myself to sleeping in the porch. I was used to it. The freezing cold porch with the sliding door that never shut properly. That had a coconut mat to wipe your feet on. That I had to use as a pillow, like a fucking prickly hedgehog stabbing into my head and ears. I hate bloody coconut anyway; this just topped it off.

I suffered that bloody spiky coconut mat only for Garry. No wonder he pissed off and left me; he obviously got fed up with my unhinged family and my possible mental issues from the constant abuse. Looking back on the situation, I couldn't blame him. I remember begging, pleading, crying at him NOT to leave me, NOT to finish with me, as I knew I would be thrown back into the lion's den. The den of physical violence, mental cruelty and hurt: THAT was my mother.

All those years ago when I was young, he was my security blanket, my saviour. With him, my life was worth living; without him, it wasn't. He had tried to take me away from it all but had failed miserably. He had looked though the *Hull Daily Mail* newspaper one night and saw a flat to rent down the Boulevard in Hull. We both went to see it. It wasn't a nice flat as it was damp with threadbare carpet, but I didn't care. At that time, Garry was an apprentice at British Aerospace and not on brilliant money. I was on even less money on a Youth Training Scheme at an independent travel agent's, and I bloody well hated it. Between us, we could afford to rent the flat, but nothing else – such as food. I again didn't care; I just wanted to leave home. We told the landlord that we were both going to think about it.

Unfortunately, after viewing the flat, we walked to the bus stop down Hessle Road and my father passed us in his car. The one and only night he went to his model railway society club down Hessle Road on a Thursday night, and he saw us stood there. Bloody typical. He stopped, and we both got into the car. He obviously asked what we were doing down Hessle Road and Garry told him. I knew it would erupt like a bloody volcano when we got back to Hessle, and it did. Firstly, because he was banned from seeing me, and vice versa, and secondly, because I shouldn't even be looking for accommodation with him.

I was seriously confused. Every day, my mother spat the words at me that I was a 'lazy, good-for-nothing layabout', yet now I was leaving home she was annoyed. She would have no one to take her anger out on anymore, no one to use as a punchbag, to punish or bully. They were both bastards – my mother and my father. He was a weak man for not stopping her punishing me. I never forgive or forget.

Garry had once bought me an eternity ring from Ratners in Hull. It was gold with garnets and cubic zirconia stones. I treasured it as if it were real diamonds, as it was the first piece of jewellery I had ever been given at the age of seventeen or eighteen. I even hid it from Mother as I knew she would possibly flush it down the toilet, just to see my reaction. I knew her evil mind. Yes, Garry and I were forever, until SHE, that bitch, split us up. I would never EVER forgive her.

SHIT! So here was Garry on the phone NOW. Sounding just the same. But we were both speaking with more articulation and clarity, not the young teenage speak and mumbling we had used forty years ago. What the heck had possessed me to contact him and intrude into his new life? I'd now forgotten. My mind had wandered as it always did; I couldn't concentrate like I used to. Oh yeah, I suddenly remembered – I was suicidal, deranged and fucking dying and needed to say goodbye.

CHAPTER 4

CHATLINES AND BLURRED LINES

I now had to cope with the true realisation of my situation. That anxiety, panic, fear, uncertain feeling ... No one knew the real stress I was having, emotionally and monetary, including the unexpected cost of the funeral. Andrew had thought he was insured – he was, but insured for accidental death, nothing else. This wasn't an accident; therefore, he wasn't insured. He had paid into a policy for years – for nothing. A big lesson learnt there. I was learning plenty of lessons now. Every day was a school day.

In the last month, his mother had been wittering on about spending hundreds of pounds for some flowers on a religious cross for Andrew's coffin. But I noticed she didn't offer to pay for it. I ignored her and paid for a bunch of white lilies, the same as we had for our wedding day in New Zealand. That would mean more to Andrew than a cross. This was Andrew's day – NOT hers. Even at her age, she was trying to take over and be in control. Andrew wasn't very religious; she hadn't a clue what he liked – I did. Little things like that now pissed me off big time. I kept thinking things over and over in my mind.

No wonder we got married abroad, so *we* had full control over OUR wedding, not her. It was our day, no one else's. We organised it, with only witnesses and a celebrant there. It was OUR decision, and the best day of our lives. She sulked, I let her. She cried and said that he was her only child. That wasn't HIS fault. It was her or her husband's fault, not Andrew's. I told her that. She needed knocking down a peg or two. Some people are just busybodies and think they are in control. Well, not anymore. Yeah, the realisation struck me that I was now all alone, and most of my close family certainly didn't care, or even want to know me. I shouldn't be shocked as I was used to that by now – but deep down, it still hurt.

The money situation scared me. I didn't even have a credit card. Andrew had one that he would use for bills. I now had no choice but to get one. Firstly, to pay the garage for our car repairs, the cost of which had accumulated to over £1,500 before Andrew died. And secondly, for the funeral and to live day to day. We had no savings as all our money had been ploughed into our old house to be renovated. A full rewire, new plumbing with a new boiler, new floorboards, walls knocked down, a new kitchen and an extension. The list went on. We both realised that we had made a bloody big mistake buying the house. Our five-year investment plans were to flip it for a profit. Ideally to renovate it, sell it and move to a nice detached bungalow and live our best lives.

The truth and reality was that the house we had bought was a hell house, a massive fucking money pit. Whatever we touched broke, or there was a problem, usually a big bloody expensive problem. The house took away our quality of life, our sanity, our time and all our money. Over the years, it nearly cost us our marriage. Other people said they would have just walked away. Unfortunately, we had nowhere to walk to, and had to ride it out – together. As the renovation work started, the costs seemed to suddenly spiral much higher than the original price quoted, as there was always an 'unforeseen problem' or an 'unexpected situation'.

We were living in the house of hell whilst the builders were renovating. There were numerous warning signs pinned up on our driveway gate stating 'Hard hats must be worn on this site at all times' and 'Danger construction site – keep out'. It was a building site, inside and out. Scaffolding was erected everywhere, floorboards pulled up, plaster hanging off the walls where wiring had been chased, walls knocked down and old red powdery brick dust was everywhere. We had no wardrobes or cupboards; our clothes that were stored in boxes were now covered in brick dust.

The house was now a death trap. WE were now living in that death trap, the builder quite blasé about the warning signs: 'Oh, they're only up for the public, you know, to make them aware.' However, we still persevered, thinking it would get better in time. I wanted to move; I couldn't stand it any longer. The constant lack of privacy of having builders and tradesmen in the house, or not at all if they couldn't be bothered to turn up, was stressful.

I was used to having no running water and having to wee behind the shed, even in the middle of the night, even if it was raining or snowing. It became the norm. It was a luxury to have just one tap connected so I could wash my brick dust-coated hair in a cold bucket of water. I may as well have turned back the clock and gone back in time to our old decrepit caravan at Hornsea from the 1970s, with no running water, no bathroom and no electricity. This was exactly the same situation, and I bloody hated it. The neighbours were now complaining about overflowing skips and possible vermin. The builders were noisy, sometimes putting their radio on loud and shouting to each other, then the banging and drilling early in the morning. No wonder some neighbours complained and we argued. Looking back – I don't bloody blame them. I probably would have done the same.

After a few years of living like this, I had seriously had enough and used to wake up crying, wishing I could turn the clock back and live in a normal house like we used to, with floorboards, walls and warm running water with a toilet that flushed. I didn't ask for much in life. But still we stayed strong together, knowing that one day this hell would be over and we could move on. When we got fed up waiting for the tradesmen to arrive, we had to do things ourselves. That was a killer. I was working full time and out of the area, coming back home at 6pm, then working renovating the house until gone midnight. Waking up at 5am to start the mundane process – all over again.

Plastering, painting, laying floorboards, laying carpets, moving tonnes of aggregate from front to the back garden all by wheelbarrow, laying pathways in the back garden; you name it – we did it. We were fast learners; after all, we had no choice. I had to do the majority of work as Andrew was suddenly becoming weaker and more tired as the months went by. The hired concrete mixer was constantly working, along with the wacker plate and other plant and machinery. WE were constantly working – even on Christmas Day. Whatever day it was, it didn't matter – it needed doing. JFDI was our saying – J*ust Fucking Do It.* No one else cared or helped; we had no money left to pay them – it was us against the world, yet again.

Andrew and I made a good team. We were both quite methodical; after all, the end goal was for both of us. But as time went on, I began to resent people coming to the house. I was shattered and tired beyond belief, and I was still driving to Leeds and back every day for work. The whole project after five years eventually took its toll even more. The builder had gone bust and left the country, the window company had gone bust, the electrician had a massive argument and the first plumber had gotten into a strop and yanked all his pipework up from the floorboards and threatened to firebomb the house. This was now a regular occurrence in this house. Death threats, crying, arguments, shouting and some bloody drama or damage. The house from fucking hell. I was absolutely pissed off and would have gladly just left it all behind, even made a loss, I just didn't care; I was past caring. But this was OUR investment. Surely it would get better? I was secretly praying it WOULD bloody get better as I wasn't sure how much more I could take. It never. In fact, it got progressively worse.

So here I was now, eight years later, living in a house that still needed completing. Broken windows and doors were now the norm; in fact, broken anything was now the norm. Even my bloody divan bed was broken, as well as my heart. I couldn't even sell the house in the state it was in. I had to carry on and think of another way of getting quick money for house repairs, and to live. Randomly, I chose the Chatlines.

CHAPTER 5

SEX CHATS AND FANNY FLAPS

The chatlines seemed an easy option. I think the next step would have possibly been prostitution. I was seriously past fucking caring anymore. I researched it and thought about it – the good and bad, the situations, how to act, what men could ask, etc. I had never called a chatline so didn't have a bloody clue.

There was nothing out there on Google or YouTube of any actual conversation on a chatline. I only found one random YouTube video of an American lady on the phone to a client. You could only hear her – not him. She was slapping her thigh as if she was being slapped on her face, and pretending to have an orgasm. She was shouting at the client to stop slapping her and stop pulling her hair. OH MY GOD! This now looked very intense and overwhelming. The lady on the phone sounded loud and brash. I wasn't. She gave an excellent performance. I was now a bit scared, but I had to think of the 'bigger picture' as they say ... and the 'bigger picture' and end solution to this whole travesty – was money. I had to learn to be a good actress, as she certainly was one.

I took a step back and worked things out logically on paper. I was a project manager by profession. I had to be realistic and analyse everything, from the time I would be on the chatlines to the profit I could make. I had to treat it as a business and it had to be a viable solution; otherwise, I may as well just give it all up along with the house, and let it become repossessed by the mortgage company. Then where would I live? Possibly on the streets. I had to get fucking real with this; it was a matter of sink or swim. I'm not even a very strong swimmer, but I soon would be.

I worked out the maximum I could charge per minute on the chatlines. Monetary limits were set by the company. If I did well, over a few months, then I could increase my prices per minute. If I charged maximum £1 a minute, that would be £60 an hour, less the chatline company's commission and my tax. It was a very good hourly rate. In my usual job, I was on the IT helpdesk, talking all day long. To be truthful, I was actually 'out of conversation' after a full day at work and didn't particularly want to talk anymore after hours of talking. But now I had no choice. Talking or eviction ...? That was the choice – no choice.

The business side seemed easy; it was the small talk that wasn't. In my mind, I thought I was prepared for the sexy small talk, almost forgetting I had been married for many years and any sexy talk sort of fizzles out after the honeymoon period. To be honest, even sex fizzles out after the two-week honeymoon period! After years of our traumatic house dramas, the thought of sexual talk, or the act of making love, just faded away, never to come back again. We were both just too tired and stressed for sex.

So here I was now, on my computer, online, registering for the chatlines, filling in my name, address, bank account and tax details. I couldn't look back; this HAD to happen. I needed to keep the hell house, for my sake and Andrew's sake. How could I let it be repossessed after he had worked so hard at his businesses to pay for it? How could I let him and myself down? I couldn't – this was bloody going ahead, and I was going to have to learn to be an extremely good actress.

I completed the registration forms and luckily could use a false name for the clients and for my profile page. I chose a name that I liked, one I wished I had been called when I was born, not a boring name like 'Helen'. I looked at the other women's profiles to get an idea of what to even write on my page. They were all younger than I was. Shit – I was at a disadvantage already. Although some of their photos left a lot to be desired, not even matching underwear. I knew I could do better than those photos with my own selfies. I was no oil painting, I knew that, so I would just have to try even harder.

I cringed as I wrote about myself, but no one knew me, so what did it matter? It didn't. I wrote that I was a MILF (Mother I'd Like to Fuck) and said I liked younger men, which was a massive lie as Andrew was a couple of years older than me. To me, MILF meant I was bloody old, wrinkly, doddery and possibly with some ailment like arthritis. But I went with the current terms, which were allegedly horny to younger men. I sighed and uploaded a photo of myself onto the chatlines website along with, for good measure, some photos of my feet in classy high-heeled shoes. I guessed that was what most men liked visually. I really hadn't a clue. But my feet were slim, plus looked better than other parts of my overweight and wrinkly body.

I had a degree in Business Management but had never used it to my advantage. I had always been passed over for promotion at work to other people who hadn't as many qualifications. Well, bollocks to that and them, as now I WOULD be using it, especially the marketing module on promoting products. I would now promote myself as a tart – THAT was my product. My Unique Selling Point. A product – at a price. I began taking more photos, being careful to hide the flabby, floppy bits of my body that I seemed to have acquired since moving into the house of hell and not having time for the gym anymore.

I clicked on the next page of the registration process. Bloody hell, I now needed to record two voice messages for the clients to listen to. One recording had to be 'tame', the other 'explicit', then clients chose which one they wanted when they called me. I had to write down what I wanted to say as I hadn't much idea. There was a demo recording to listen to – Oh My God! I was stunned at the sexual language I had just heard. Was it a chatline or a brothel? I was going to have to just fucking do it. JFDI, I told myself. I started with the explicit voice message as I could be dramatic, swearing and just shouting random sexual words. The swearing came naturally nowadays. In fact, every other word that came out of my mouth was a swear word. I almost had my own language – Swear-a-lot. Possibly from exasperation at my situation and 'I just do not give a fuck anymore'. I listened back to my recording – I sounded like a dominatrix – swearing, hard and demanding. Yes, that would do. I was now seriously past caring.

The tame message was a bit harder to record. I just pretended I had a girly voice – which is hard to do when you have a naturally bellowing, assertive voice. I sounded like a blooming shouting Barbie. It took a few attempts to talk more slowly, more suggestively, and with calmness. But I managed it and saved the recordings. Secretly cringing to myself, but I knew I didn't have any choice at that precise time. I had to treat this as if I were an actor and this was a business. Those words meant nothing to me in my real life. I also knew I was way out of my depth, and I certainly wasn't comfortable being uncomfortable. I had to learn, and learn bloody quickly.

A few days later, all of the website security checks had been done and confirmed, and a passcode was sent to me to activate my chatlines page. I set my phone link on my iPad to 'active' and waited, almost scared to answer it if it rang.

The first conversation I had on the chatline was horrendous. Not quite like the IT helpdesk I was used to. There were no set questions – and certainly no set answers. I liked routine, and this certainly wasn't routine. It was just random sexual words along with questions about the intimate areas of my body, along with rude, crude talk from men and what they wanted to do to me.

Shit, this was harder than I thought. I had had no training; this was a different world of sex talk. It seemed that everyone on the chatlines could speak rude and vulgar easily – all except me! Another book to write for me: *How to Act and Talk on Chatlines,* I thought.

I later sat down and thought about my way forward with the chatlines. I HAD to improve and learn to talk quieter – men didn't particularly want to hear my loud voice, with a Hull accent, on the telephone. It wasn't exactly a turn-on; I had to calm it down a bit. Time WAS money; I had to learn to speak more slowly and seductively on the phone. This went against all my principles, but stuff it, it was an act and nothing else. I also had to learn more about sex – and quickly!

The first time a man rang and asked me to have an orgasm, I nearly fell off my chair in the room! All my calmness suddenly disappeared, and I almost ended up hyperventilating. How the hell was I going to do THAT on the phone? I wasn't used to having an orgasm; in fact, I couldn't even remember the last time I had even had a bloody orgasm! I certainly hadn't had time for orgasms over the past few years. My world hadn't been about sex and orgasms; it had been about renovating a house, cooking, cleaning, being a carer and wiping arses.

So here I was, sat in my spare bedroom being asked to perform an orgasm on the phone. Shit, this was seriously getting out of hand – in more ways than one! I certainly wouldn't be bringing myself to an orgasm, so I was going to have to make some pretend noises – and bloody quick! I had even forgotten the man's name on the phone with the shock of it all. Oh well, I would just call him 'Babe'. That would have to do. To me, Babe was a really cute sheep-pig in a film that I enjoyed in the 1990s. Well, today, that name belonged to a man, not a sheep-pig or a talking piglet. You couldn't make this shit up.

I suddenly remembered the scene from the film *When Harry Met Sally* and she had a pretend screaming orgasm in a restaurant. I would have to do the same. After all, time is money, and I desperately needed the money.

I began with a few words of 'Oh, babe ...' and tried not to think of the sheep-pig. He replied that he already had his cock out and it was in his hand, hard and ready to cum. He wanted to AND needed to cum – NOW! I was secretly mortified. Shit. There were long pauses as he obviously wanted me to take the lead whilst he just silently played with himself. Okay, I told myself, I was going to have to just go for it and pretend I was having an orgasm. All the phone calls were recorded, which made me feel under even more pressure. But I knew what this was all about when I signed up for it, so let's get this fake orgasm out of the way and move on to the next caller.

My act continued with slowly sighing and gradually building up to a bit of gasping and panting. I threw a few verbal 'oh fucks' in, just to encourage the situation. It possibly sounded more like I was having contractions and about to give birth to a 10lb baby than having an orgasm. My moaning continued, and I dreaded it in case my next-door neighbours could hear me. But I remembered that 'time was money' and could see the clock on the chatlines page on my iPad showing the minutes on the call. I was now calculating in my head how much I charged per minute and multiplying it by the time spent on this call. Yeah, now he could bloody well wait for ME to finish. More time – more money. I was now in control – not him.

The gasping and animal noises continued. This now possibly sounded like a scene from the film *Babe,* the sheep-pig on the farmyard. Or was it Old MacDonald's farm? Who knew? I certainly bloody didn't anymore! I kept on grunting, along with a few 'ooh babe … I'm going to cum, MAKE me cum' shout-outs. In a strange way, I actually wished I would hurry up and bloody cum, as my throat was getting sore from all the gasping and strange noises I had been making intermittently over the last ten minutes or so. I really needed a drink of water, but I could hardly stop this monologue and say in my best Hull accent, 'Oh, just a minute, babe, hold onto your cock a bit longer. I need a glass of water.' I would let him dangle (literally) for a bit longer …

I eventually let out an explosive scream that even shocked myself, possibly sounding more like an animal in pain. He took that to be an orgasm. I didn't know whether to applaud myself at the end of that Oscar-winning performance, or just go and get a glass of water. He had obviously cum and already put the phone down. I obviously hadn't cum. It was bloody hard work having to talk through an orgasm, every step of the way, what I was doing, what I wanted him to do, exaggerate every noise. I was worn out. It was more tiring than having an actual bloody real orgasm, from what I could remember!

I also had to learn to be a hard bitch and not let any criticism upset me. One man rang me and asked where I was from. I replied 'Yorkshire' and he slammed the phone down. I was mortified as I wondered if he hated my accent, or had someone just walked in and caught him on his phone? I would never know. But I do know that in just those few seconds I made about 25p. Therefore, win-win. Beggars couldn't be choosers.

A few weeks later, I was used to talking explicitly and was now prepared as best I could be, using flip-chart paper to write down sexual words and phrases, so I didn't even have to think. It became easier as time went on. I treated it like *Jackanory* – the television programme for children many years ago. After all, I was really telling a story that had a beginning, middle and an end. The end was always predictable in my case – male ejaculation, a bloody massive climax. It was more like 'Jack-off-a-nory'! It was laughable, but at the same time it wasn't. People were paying for this service; I had to make it bloody good.

I had now created a comment-bank, or what I could call a 'comment-wank', or words, phrases and acronyms, words I would never even have dreamt of. Heaven help me if anyone looked at my internet search engine history on my computer at home. There were words I couldn't even spell or pronounce. I had missed out on all this sexual lingo and abbreviations. I had been married faithfully for thirteen years, and we certainly didn't do sex talk. In fact, I was embarrassed with my body. Goodness knows what Andrew would have thought if he could see me now. I know with his business brain he possibly wouldn't have minded; we were both always making money in one way or another, thinking ahead, earning and selling things. Well, now I was selling something – my online sexual services.

However, I could now feel slight resentment creeping in. If Andrew had left insurance policies, then I wouldn't be doing this. Other people who were widowed would be living a good life with no money worries. A good insurance payout, paying off the mortgage, bills and loans. Living a life of luxury with the windfall of insurance. But not me, not ever. I knew that if I had died first then Andrew would have had a good secure life, as I had numerous insurance policies, death in service benefits and pensions. Everything would be paid off and he would have been able to afford proper care for his disabilities. But now look at it! My life was the total opposite. I was skint and had now sexually gone from one extreme to another – I had changed from a chatline virgin to a chatline whore in only a few weeks! I wasn't sure if I should laugh or cry. I had become hardened to any emotion and was now out of emotion. I just carried on regardless. I shouldn't feel resentful. Andrew and I had had a good life; this was now just a *different* life.

*

I was sat up in bed in my spare bedroom, talking on the chatlines. I was wearing my snuggly, warm fleecy pyjamas and watching television. It was on mute but with subtitles. My duvet was pulled over me to keep me warm.

'Ooh what am I wearing? ... Babe, I am wearing a black see-through bra and black lacy panties ... yes, you CAN see my nipples through my bra ... do you like big breasts and big nipples?'

For goodness' sake! I had easily learnt to talk in a sexually explicit way. It was unbelievable, and now bordering on being uncouth and vulgar. My comment-wank flip-chart paper was now stuck up on the walls of my spare bedroom, and I could now lay in bed and just read out any relevant phrases or words without really thinking. I just mixed and matched any sexual words, anything really that sounded good. My explicit describing words were now excellent, deserving of an A* grade in an English Language exam, and definitely A* in an English Oral exam.

This was my project management skills to the bloody extreme. Meticulously thought-out and detailed. I wasn't sure if I was a good project planner or just a sad twat on the chatlines! My lines and principles were definitely blurred in many ways. I had now managed my big project, although I am sure that any project planners would be horrified at me using my planning methods for the chatlines. But, like I was told in my project training and my qualifications twenty-four years ago, 'The Prince2 methodology can be applied to any suitable situation in life where you have to confidently achieve an end result within a given timescale'. Well, here I was – confidently achieving that end result. Reading scripts and monologues on the chatlines, and changing the chats to what I wanted – not them. I was now having 'easy cum – easy go' telephone conversations that were manageable and relaxed. Throw in a few 'change requests' along the way – and I had a quick turnover of satisfied clients.

But still the men shocked me; they were so random with their questions. 'Have you got big fanny flaps?' one man asked me. What the hell? Did he mean the labia? Did he mean the outer or inner labia? I think I was looking too much into this situation with my limited anatomical knowledge. I had only learnt basic anatomy in my level 3 Personal Trainer exam many years ago. I could name some basic muscles and bones, and even the endocrine system, but certainly didn't know much about the vagina and its structure. I somehow don't think that was on the training course. Or, if it was, I must have been absent for that module! So, here I was now, talking fanny flaps, also known to other people as 'labia'. I quickly grabbed my spare iPad and began googling 'labia sizes' – yes, they came in all sizes apparently … ! I honestly didn't know that. But I do now.

However, did he like big fanny flaps or small fanny flaps? I hadn't a clue how to respond. Did I say yes or no? I deflected the question back onto him. 'Babe … do YOU like big fanny flaps?'

'Yeah – I fucking DO!' he replied in a deep voice.

'Oh babe, that's okay then …' I sighed calmly '… as I DO have big fanny flaps and they are wide open, just waiting for you.' The words flowed out of my mouth as if it was a normal conversation. I didn't really have big fanny flaps, no bigger than any other woman's flaps. But the customer is always right, so yes, just this once, I DID have his big flipping and flapping fantasy fanny flaps!

CHAPTER 6

LET ME BE YOUR FANTASY

'Hostage Man' subscribed to my chatlines, paying £20 a month. I used this to my advantage and sent him some free photos and additional photos he had to pay extra for. It was a nice little earner. We sent messages through the Chatlines website to each other. All was friendly and he said he was a lorry driver and just needed someone to 'chat' to at the end of his long day. We arranged to talk at certain times of the night.

He said he was into bondage; I acted like I was too. But I was out of my depth yet again. He told me his fantasy was me knocking on his door at home and then kidnapping him. Although I thought this was rather bizarre, I didn't want to lose him as a client, as he was paying good money. I decided to go along with it; after all, it was only telephone talk. There was no actual kidnapping taking place.

He sent me a message with a script attached to it. This was about four pages long; he called it a role-play script that he wanted us to act out over the phone. I printed it out and read it. It was really detailed; this was beginning to sound like an amateur porn film, but also a bit dark.

The detailed scenario was that my car had allegedly broken down outside his house. I had to knock on his door and tell him my dilemma. He would invite me in and make me a cup of tea. He would telephone someone to help with my car. I would reach into my handbag and take out a red silky scarf and a small bottle of perfume, asking him to sniff the perfume that I'd dabbed onto the silky scarf. But it wasn't perfume; it was chloroform. I would then sedate him with this and tie his hands together, eventually putting him into the back seat of my car, sedating him even more and driving (my car miraculously now working) onto the motorway and then on to some secluded wooded area. Here, I would tie him up even more, shove my red panties in his mouth, tease him and give him oral sex then eventually full sex.

This bizarre script went on and on. But in my head this was business with no emotion. I knew I'd be getting quite a bit of money for this, even if I charged 50p a minute. I was hoping we'd be on the phone for nearly an hour, win-win. If I could charge £1 a minute then even better. I had learnt to be a good actress. I wasn't keen with the chloroform reference, but it was only role play, so I put it to the back of my mind and just thought of the money.

He sent requests for numerous photos. I was now used to taking selfies of myself in bizarre situations. Rolling about on the grass in my garden – half naked. Locked in the dog's cage at home. Dressed up as a slut. I didn't care anymore. Hostage Man asked for a photo of a red silky scarf with a bottle of perfume and a photo of me driving on the motorway with him allegedly tied up on the back seat. I now needed props. I needed to make this realistic. I went to local charity shops and found a red silky scarf; well, it was actually cheap polyester and cost £1, but it would do. I got into my husband's massive black expensive Range Rover Evoque, the sporty version with black tinted windows. I parked up safely at some nice local wooded area (like in his fantasy) near the local alpaca farm, and took plenty of photos of me sitting in the front seat of the car. The woman working at the alpaca farm must have thought I was bloody crazy. She possibly wouldn't be wrong there. I was beginning to enjoy this just a bit too much, but it was easy money, and that was my end goal – money.

I had a nice pale blue flowery dress on with my cleavage showing. I took selfie shots of me behind the steering wheel and on the back seat with the caption 'I can't wait to tie you up on here'. The photos went on and on. I even threw some thick blue rope on the back seat of the car to tantalise him more. I was determined to make this realistic; after all, the Range Rover needed a good run out anyway on the M62. I had to think of some other benefit to this fantasy, which was now running out of control.

Our chat went ahead as planned. Some photos had been sent in advance, and I just knew Hostage Man would be gagging for it. He had already paid for, and downloaded, the photos. The role play went ahead, and my acting and voice skills astounded even myself. I was using props to encourage it even more. I was clinking and squirting bottles of perfume, and letting him imagine I was dealing with chloroform, jangling car keys when it came to the part about putting him in the back of my car. After nearly an hour, Hostage Man had a wank and went, thanking me for my role play. He would send another script for next week. 'Okay, babe, I will look forward to it,' I replied. I had made more money in that hour, talking and sending photos, than I would have done for a full eight hours on the helpdesk at my usual place of work. However, I just knew it was too good to be bloody true! And it was.

Two days later, I got an email from the chatline company. I knew it was bad news when the subject header of the email was 'Kidnapping fantasy and drugging him at 7.40pm'.

Apparently, I had contravened most of their company rules and regulations by enticing a hostage and kidnapping situation, along with encouraging substance abuse. Any more of this behaviour and I would be reported to the FBI (obviously an American chatline company). I was now on a warning and being monitored. For goodness' sake!

I rang them and explained it was only role play and no one was being kidnapped or sniffing chloroform. After all, wasn't that the point of chatlines – to talk and act out their fantasies? No, apparently not. I had breached most of their regulations in that one hour and was on a first warning. Bloody hell, it was like being at work on my usual helpdesk shift with every phone call recorded and listened to. But I needed the money, and they did pay me for that call, so all was good. Unfortunately, when Hostage Man sent me another bizarre script, I had to decline, therefore losing money – I was fuming. Never mind chatlines, this was now the bloody twat-lines! But I suppose rules are rules, however ridiculous they might be.

I would give the chatlines a break and pick it up again near Christmas time. I needed a break from it all.

CHAPTER 7

LITTLE LIES

My life-saving operation was booked in for the end of September. I felt more panic and anxiety and felt I needed to enjoy life before it was too late. Time was slipping through my fingers – too bloody quickly.

Tinder became a bit of a stupid habit, but it entertained me after work. It had the same people on there, fake photos and fake write-ups. Even reading their profiles had me in stitches of laughter, and that was even before my operation. Most profiles from men were ridiculous, exaggerated and written to catfish women. With them getting off on the idea of meeting a random woman and having sex immediately, but they would never go through with it, and I knew that. All a great big fantasy, like they probably saw on porn on the internet.

One profile was from a man in the Chapeltown area of Leeds. I didn't know every area of Leeds well, but knew of Chapeltown. Goodness knows how I 'matched' with his profile, but men just added every hobby so they would be sure to 'match' with someone. Oh, and don't forget the 'animal lover' captions also. As they think every woman likes a man who loves animals or has a dog. I certainly didn't. I could easily play that game but didn't have the time. The guy from Chapeltown messaged me: Take some photos of you *in a mini skirt*. I laughed to myself but did a skirt-and-leg shot. That was all I showed; no face, and definitely no pussy, just skirt. *Fuck, I want to meet you,* he messaged.

I replied later that night, *If we meet, it has to be somewhere public for a coffee or a drink, in a café or pub.*

The conversation continued with him adamant we should meet in 'private'. I deflected his insistence on meeting in private. He asked if I had a car. I replied that I did. That confirmation, unfortunately, encouraged him even more. *Come and collect me from my flat*, he requested. I knew this was not going to happen.

I messaged back, *Oh, where would you like to go? After all, it is bank holiday soon.*

He replied, *I want you to wear that miniskirt and no knickers, then drive me into some woods in Leeds, and I will rape you. I bet you would like that.*

I sighed to myself and said out loud, 'Yeah, sure, that is just the kind of man I want to meet ... what a loser.' I went to block his profile, but suddenly his profile disappeared from Tinder, as if by magic – no surprise there then. What a total and utter knobhead. Oh well, I hope he enjoyed the photo of my legs. I didn't let their fantasy shit get to me.

Another man messaged me on Tinder. The 'match' was due to both our jobs in computers. I had kept my profession vague – 'computers' covered a multitude of things. He then confessed that he was a computer hacker. I asked more questions. Was he a legitimate hacker, like some large companies employ to ensure their systems can't be hacked? I asked many questions, probably too many for his liking, such as: didn't the company he worked for have cyber security, encryption, virus protection, back-ups, etc? I somehow knew the answers before I even asked them. He said he was employed by a worldwide company but worked from home – after all, he said, that is how hackers work. I could have said so much more; I had worked in IT for over twenty-five years and wasn't exactly naïve when it came to computers, servers and security. He didn't know this fact, but I think he was getting edgy, so I let it drop.

I was getting bored anyway with Computer Hacker Man's alleged lies, but still he persisted. He asked me, *Do you want to meet at TGI Fridays at Birstall near where I live?* My heart sank as I didn't really want to drive all that way, plus there was usually traffic queuing for the massive Ikea based there, but I perked up when I remembered there were other shops on the shopping park and a cinema.

Ok then, I replied by text, sighing to myself, especially because it was a bank holiday weekend and it would be exceptionally busy. I seriously couldn't be bothered with it all now. He had pushed me too far with his so-called hacking lies. He went ahead and planned arrangements for a meet-up, but I somehow felt uneasy. I didn't want to go.

I messaged my friend Suzanne for a second opinion; she was a good judge of character and always calm and rational – unlike me. I sent her a photo of the Tinder man, the so-called hacker. She replied telling me to stay well away. Yeah, I had that feeling too.

Suddenly he messaged me again: *I don't think it is a good idea to meet in a public place, too many people know me. Why don't you come to mine instead? I will cook a meal and we would have more privacy, and you could stay the night.*

THAT definitely wasn't happening! The goalposts had been moved again. One minute we were supposed to be going out for a meal, the next we were having a meal at his house, and I was allegedly staying the night. I certainly wouldn't be staying at a random's house overnight. I blocked him from my Tinder profile. I really despaired of them all; it was all their fantasies and no reality. But that's the hinder of Tinder, I suppose. I now had to concentrate on myself and my imminent operation.

CHAPTER 8

ONE-NIGHT STAND

Private healthcare saved my life. No one else did. I owe my life to one person – the consultant, the only person who believed me, and diagnosed me. For which I will be eternally grateful. The tumour was large; I was cut down my body and straight through my belly button. I knew I would be scarred for life and now had a wonky belly button, but in the grand scheme of things, what did that matter? I was alive and had been given a second chance of life; I wasn't going to waste it.

In my now unusual and extreme world, nearly every day was like Christmas Day. Instead of unwrapping presents, I was undressing men. It was the same thing to me. Something new, tempting, dangerous and exciting, and all just for me. My own personal presents; after all, I now had no one to buy for, or give me any gifts in return.

Simon was another Tinder hook-up. We began messaging each other early autumn. He seemed to have a similar sense of humour as myself – if I had one left after this year's trauma. Tinder didn't have the best-looking blokes, and he certainly wasn't that attractive, but then neither was I. I was honest with him and told him I was going into hospital for an urgent operation, so if he was looking for sex he would have to wait, possibly until December when I had healed. I had no shame anymore. I wasn't even sure if I would survive the operation.

It was now the beginning of December and Simon messaged again, asking to meet up. I needed to know more about him, as he now seemed a bit more reserved than he was initially with his flirty messages and chat a few months previously. He confessed he had been on Tinder for years, single, and was only 'looking for fun'. Telling me randomly, almost to reassure me, about his sexual conquests. He had recently messaged a woman on Tinder. Half an hour later, she was at his flat having sex, and then he paid for a taxi for her to go straight back home. Alarm bells were ringing in my head, but I dismissed them, as this seemed to be the norm for some men on Tinder.

I had already booked an overnight stay in a hotel in Leeds, for myself, as a Christmas treat after my operation. If Simon wanted to come and stay over, he could; I wasn't really that bothered. I had planned to go Christmas shopping in Leeds and then have a nice meal, alone. Being alone didn't bother me. In fact, I now liked my own company better than being with some of these random men; it gave me thinking time.

I arrived in Leeds at lunchtime and went to the main shopping area for a mooch around, before checking into the hotel. Simon eventually turned up and met me in the hotel room, late afternoon. I admit that I did feel like a bit of a tart, almost like a prostitute, opening the room door with a plastic beaker full of champagne in my hand. I had brought my own mini-bar with me, which included champagne and cans of cider. I wasn't paying those extortionate hotel mini-bar prices. I poured him a drink of cider, as he didn't apparently like champagne, and I also gave him a jokey Christmas card. I had made an effort, ordering a personalised card from Moonpig. I needn't have bothered. He had brought nothing in return, just himself and a manky rucksack with a change of clothes in it. I ignored and dismissed his rudeness. Even a box of chocolates would have been nice as a small Christmas gift. I looked at him and sighed. No wonder he was bloody single; he hadn't a clue how to treat women. The idiot, he should have been called 'Simple Simon'.

We got down to business straight away on the large super king-sized bed. I guessed from his performance that he had taken Viagra, as the session continued for almost two hours. I was still recovering from my operation and shouldn't have been having sex so soon afterwards. I was worried in case my newly healed stitches popped open from the momentum, but I put that thought to the back of my mind and carried on. My consultant from the hospital would be mortified as he had advised me to 'take things easy'. I didn't dare ask what type of 'easy' things he meant. I wasn't sure if sex was one of them. I felt he was too posh for me to ask such a ridiculous question. I had just had a life-saving operation; I could hardly say to him in my best posh Hull accent, 'Oh, and by the way – just when do you think I WILL be able to have sexual intercourse safely again?' Therefore, I was going ahead with this crazy one-night stand. This was one of my Christmas presents to myself, and I was determined to bloody enjoy it.

Afterwards, we both got showered and dressed smartly and went into Leeds city centre for a meal and a few drinks. Simon seemed distant and I got the feeling he now didn't want to be there. I didn't really care if he either stayed or went home; it was his choice. I told him that he could always get the train to wherever he lived (somewhere in West Yorkshire) and just walk away from this night out. However, I would be staying, whatever he decided. He dismissed my comments by saying, 'Don't be silly, it's cool.' But I knew it wasn't, and back at the hotel we kept to our own sides of the bed all night, both catnapping until the early hours of the morning.

The next morning, we ate breakfast in the hotel restaurant together, but there was an awkward silence, him having to go outside to make a phone call to work – allegedly. We both walked the short distance to Leeds train station and parted company, and I knew this had been a big mistake and a big lesson learnt. Even my bloody train had been cancelled to add to the stress and stupidity of the whole situation. I sat on the next train in a daze, annoyed with myself.

That night, Simon texted me. Telling me it felt 'sleazy'. I responded curtly with the truth. It was HIM that had instigated this, not me. I also reminded him politely that it was HIM that had a sleazy Tinder hook-up with another woman within a few minutes of messaging her online, had sex, and then tossed her aside. I asked him if that was a lie. I never received an answer to those questions. Bye-bye, Simple Simon.

To add to the stress, on my return home, I immediately received a phone call from the hospital where Sheila, Andrew's mum, had recently been admitted. She had now been transferred to yet another hospital as she was still very ill. I couldn't visit her as there were still COVID restrictions in place. I felt guilty hooking up with a random man from Tinder; it seemed disrespectful and almost shameful, but I also needed a distraction away from all the doom and gloom over the past few months. I wanted to run away from it all, as I knew deep down that Sheila hadn't long to live; I dreaded hearing the inevitable news. I certainly didn't have the mental capacity or strength to cope.

CHAPTER 9

BOTOX AND BLOW JOBS

I was nearly done with my 'rounds' on Tinder. There was no one new or attractive online, and I was bored. I should really have been recovering from my major operation and abstaining from sex in an attempt to heal, but I couldn't help myself. I logged on and suddenly saw John's profile. He was younger than me, single, and from Hull with young children. I personally wouldn't have put that fact on Tinder, but at least he was honest, or maybe just naïve. I didn't care which.

He was in his late thirties, but I didn't even care about the age difference of about twenty years. We exchanged messages, him telling me that he was often away offshore. I wasn't really reading his messages; I was too busy looking at his profile picture and private dick pics he had sent me. They looked very nice and tasty. He FaceTimed me at inappropriate moments, such as in the shower, but he also made me laugh for all the right reasons. I just knew I had to meet him and see him in the flesh – literally.

We originally arranged to meet in Beverley. Unfortunately, he unexpectedly cancelled at the last minute. For goodness' sake! I had arranged time off work and had to rearrange my plans. I told him abruptly that it was an inconvenience. I gave him a warning shot that his behaviour was not acceptable, as I had a very busy diary and had to rearrange clients. However, secretly I didn't really mind as I had already arranged for an appointment to have Botox the next week. This was the first time I had ever had Botox, so it could surely only improve my looks, and I'd look even better for John. The last six months of crying, sobbing, weeping and wailing had taken its toll, and I now had bags under my eyes and not so much 'laughter lines' but 'sobbing lines', which were now big bloody creases of skin on my face.

The Botox lady lived locally and was up for anything I wanted, obviously within reason. I asked her to sort out my now wrinkly-looking eyes and my creased forehead, which had now become a permanent frown. Botox Lady explained about fillers and injections and the cost. She said she could 'iron my face to make it look nice and smooth'. I said to just do it, and whilst she was at it, sort out my thin lips. Stuff the cost; add it to my debt. She would need a very hot steam iron to iron out the frowns on my face. Or even one of those trouser presses you see in hotel rooms that get rid of creases – just stick my head in it, end of. The laughable thing was that Andrew and I always slated people on the television that had Botox, him telling me that I didn't need it. Well, ironically, because of him, I now blooming well did need it! That just shows that you should never judge. Another life lesson learnt in my state of grief.

Botox Lady proceeded to give me some injections in my face, then handed me a small cosmetic mirror so I could see the immediate results. My eyes were suddenly looking more open, although some of the treatment, she explained, would not show for maybe ten to fifteen days. I didn't care – I had lived with this crinkly, wrinkly face for many years, so a couple more weeks wouldn't matter. Even my lips looked better and plumper. The only problem was that I found I couldn't speak properly; my lips would not close together like they used to, and I now had a bit of a lisp. This was going to be a major problem, as I had to constantly speak on the phone at work, and facilitate IT training sessions. Clearly, I was not impressed by this fact, but Botox Lady explained that my lips would reduce a bit in size so not to worry.

I went home and then realised that the normal function of drinking was affected. Now I could hardly drink properly out of a cup. It was like I had had an anaesthetic at the dentist and couldn't feel my lips. I hoped this would wear off before the rearranged hot date with John.

John and I met early one afternoon in Beverley at the train station. I had taken the afternoon off work on holiday leave and was dressed up, with full make-up on with additional lip gloss, to enhance my pouty blow-job lips. I was wearing tight jeans that were hurting me across my stomach scars. But that certainly wasn't going to stop me enjoying myself. 'Nothing ventured, nothing gained' as they say. Just waking up from the operation was a miracle; I was now grabbing every opportunity and chance that I could.

We started drinking in Bartipi, which is a temporary bar inside an actual tepee, erected each year in Flemingate in preparation for Christmas celebrations. We started on cocktails. Unfortunately, I couldn't even drink my cocktail through the straw; my lips felt stiff and numb. I had to slurp the drink. Goodness knows what John must have thought of me. I managed to drink two cocktails in quick succession by holding the straw at a very strange angle in an attempt to suck up the drink.

In my head, I could remember Andrew saying to me, *Never drink alcohol through a straw as you WILL get drunk quicker*. Always quoting that fact after he used to run a hotel/pub in Dorset and had seen it happen to many people. I used to mock him for that, not believing it was true. Well, it bloody well was; and here I was myself, drinking through a straw and getting very drunk very quickly.

Bartipi was getting a bit chilly inside the tent in the late afternoon, even though there was a warm fire pit inside it. We both decided to get warmed up and ventured to the Sports Bar opposite, to continue drinking. We ordered Peronis in bottles. Unfortunately, as I took a swig, the contents spilled straight down my top. I couldn't even tell if my lips were on the bottle. My blooming 'blow-job lips'! They looked brilliant, but I still could not speak coherently, and certainly not drink properly. I now had to use a straw to even drink my Peroni. John must have thought I was a crazy boozy bitch, old enough to be his mother, dressed like a hooker with blow-job lips. But at least I had a nice smooth forehead, and no creases around my eyes. I had to go with the flow – *life is too short*, I kept telling myself silently, almost to convince myself of what I wanted to do next.

John had already asked if I wanted to stay in a hotel overnight in Beverley. I wasn't sure and said I would think about it. There was the

Premier Inn nearby, but I didn't want to appear too eager. Additionally, I didn't really know him, and had to somehow get to work the next day. If I stayed over, I knew I would not be in a fit state to work.

Six Peronis later, I was well pissed, absolutely off my head. Oh, and don't forget the two cocktails I had as starters. I couldn't even walk to the ladies' toilet in the pub without staggering into the wall. I was even laughing out loud to myself, as I needed to sober up but couldn't. In the cubicle, I tried to find some lipstick in my handbag. Goodness knows why. I certainly wasn't in a fit state to even apply any make-up, and couldn't feel my lips anyway. I couldn't find any lipstick, but the contents of my handbag spilled out onto the floor – I possibly tipped the whole lot out onto the floor. Being so drunk, I can't remember. Amongst the contents now spread across the floor was Sheila's spare keys to her flat.

Sheila had unfortunately been admitted to Hull Royal Infirmary after a bad fall and had broken her wrist. But as she had also banged her head, she was in for observation. I couldn't visit her in hospital due to hospital COVID restrictions, but I still made sure her flat was okay, collected her mail and made sure there was plenty of food in her freezer. I put my make-up back into my small handbag and tried to smile with my puffy lips. I knew what I wanted, and John was about to find out.

I staggered from the toilets to the small booth where John and I had been sitting. I had a plan in my head. I turned to John and slurred, 'John, I have an idea. My mother-in-law lives nearby and I have her spare keys. Shall we go to her flat and grab a coffee as I need to sober up?' I then jangled the flat keys in front of his face as if I had no shame. In my mind, I knew full well that a coffee wouldn't be the only thing I would be having in that flat. He had better be bloody prepared!

I led the way out of the pub, with John following like a little lost puppy. After all, he hadn't a clue where the flat was, and the way I felt with too much alcohol – neither did I. I nearly fell in front of a car that was driving down the narrow street near Beverley Minster. I was swaying and staggering along in my own little world across the pavement and the road. It was now very dark outside, and I hadn't even a clue what time it was.

I opened the main entrance door to the flats quietly. Well, I thought I was quiet, but the reality is that I was probably falling and crashing into the heavy fire door. I then fumbled around in my handbag to find the keys to her private flat door.

We entered the flat. The flat was decorated in flowery lacy designs with doilies, and decorative plates of the Queen and royalty adorned the walls. In fact, there were sixty-six plates. I knew that, as once Sheila said she had counted them whilst she was watching television. I wished I had time to even sit and watch a television. It was a typical flat for someone of ninety-one years of age – plastic flowers in glass vases and more royal memorabilia. I went into the small kitchen, put fresh water in the kettle and put it on to boil. We would have to drink 2-in-1 coffee sachets, the dried coffee variety, as there was obviously no fresh milk. I remember making the drinks, and the coffee was still burning hot, and my lips were hurting even more with slurping the hot coffee. That's all I vaguely remember.

The next thing I can sort of recall was me attempting to do a striptease, but I couldn't get my top off in my drunken state. We went into the bedroom and had sex. Whatever had possessed me? I just don't know. Lust? Loneliness? Desperation? I had seriously lost my fucking mind, in my own sad world of grief. My life was now one of quick fixes, addictions and sexual encounters, and was rapidly spiralling out of control.

John got off me and went to the bathroom and then put the kettle on again. We had another coffee, this time in silence – the laughing, joking and flirting had suddenly stopped. We got dressed and walked back to the train station in Beverley, again not talking. I got the train home, without even a wave or goodbye from him. He went to the taxi rank at the train station and ordered a taxi to Hull. I sat on the train still drunk and trying not to fall asleep. I knew it would be the last time I would see him, and I was right, it was. I didn't even care. He sent me a text message later that night to say that he wanted to concentrate more on his children. I understood. We, wrongly or rightly, both got what we wanted from that night.

I sat at work the next day, unfazed by it all. I was more concerned about having a bad hangover, and still puffy blow-job lips, than the act of having sex with a stranger. I had a sickening feeling that I hadn't locked Sheila's flat door. SHIT! As soon as I logged off work at teatime, I drove like a mad woman to her flat. Praying that she hadn't been discharged from hospital yet. I also dreaded seeing the state of her flat.

Luckily, I HAD locked her door. However, the first thing to greet me in the kitchen was four half-empty coffee cups, and half-eaten shortbread biscuits. I suddenly remembered that I had drunkenly opened a box of shortbread but had dropped some on the floor. Crumbs were everywhere and trodden into the carpet. Shit, I had better hoover up and clean the kitchen.

The state of the kitchen was nothing compared to the state of her bedroom. The bed looked like an orgy had taken place, not that I had ever participated in an orgy. Bed sheets half pulled off the bed, and the double duvet with its flowery and lacy pattern thrown all over the floor, along with an open condom wrapper and the condom packet – for extra large men! Oh My God! I certainly couldn't remember the size, or even the position! I had to clean this mess up before anyone came in. If Sheila's carers came in, heaven help me. If Sheila had been discharged from hospital and came back to this, I would have a lot of explaining to do! As I was sure they would know that the condom wrapper certainly didn't belong to her – at the age of ninety-one!

I suddenly felt very guilty. In Sheila's front room, on top of her best china cabinet, there was a silver framed wedding photo of Andrew and me, smiling, happy together. Just look what I had fucking well done now! I had betrayed everyone, including myself. Drunkenly shagged another man, a stranger I had hooked up with from Tinder, in my mother-in-law's bed. I could joke that it was the only action that bed had ever seen in its life, but at that precise point I was beyond telling jokes.

I had no moral compass anymore, and if I did, then it certainly wasn't pointing north. It was definitely pointing bloody south. I didn't know who or what to blame; Andrew's death, Sheila's health, my health? Or an accumulation of it all? Or did I blame my grief, PTSD, or lack of any mental health support? I left the question open as I didn't know, and still don't know. In fact, there was no feasible answer or reasoning for my stupidity. What had happened, happened, and I couldn't turn back time, as much as I wanted to.

CHAPTER 10

SAVE A PRAYER

Sheila died suddenly. It was a Sunday night, mid-December 2021, almost Christmas, when I received the phone call from a registrar at Hull Royal Infirmary asking me where I was, and could I come quickly? I was at home, not exactly in Hull, and no, I couldn't get there within five minutes as he had asked. It was a physical impossibility because of the distance. I drove there as soon as I put the landline down.

With the temporary 40mph zone on the A63 and Clive Sullivan Way, along with the average speed cameras coming into Hull, it seemed like a never-ending traumatic bloody journey. I was desperately trying not to cry and holding onto my sobs, knowing that once I started crying, I wouldn't be able to see to drive properly, especially in the dark. I had asked the registrar if Sheila had already passed away. He said he couldn't tell me, but I had guessed the answer. I said if she had passed, then just to tell me, so I wouldn't drive like a lunatic to the hospital. He wouldn't elaborate; it was like pulling teeth, trying to get answers out of him. He was bloody hard work, just like most men. I didn't ask for much – just the bloody truth. Now I knew why I was still single – men were such fucking hard work.

To add to the stress and more time delays, Hull Royal Infirmary was having renovation works. I eventually parked up and had to walk even further around the building to find the temporary entrance to the hospital. This was a nightmare journey and a night of hell already; it had taken me well over an hour to get there. I had now given up panicking to get there in a hurry. Let the registrar think I wasn't coming; after all, he wasn't exactly forthcoming with any information. I seriously didn't care anymore. I managed to find the correct hospital entrance, between all the building work, to get to the lifts. The hospital lifts were always blooming slow, yet another long wait.

I found the hospital ward Sheila was on. I was taken to a side room and told she had died. They said it was possibly due to frailty and heart problems. The registrar was asking me if I wanted to see her, as she was still on the ward. 'Well, it's a bit late now, isn't it?' I said to him. 'It's a bit ironic that I couldn't visit her before due to COVID, but now she IS dead, I can suddenly see her?' He politely ignored my question, or rather my angry sarcastic comment. Whatever way you look at it, though, it's a fact.

A nurse took me to see Sheila; they had closed the curtains around her bed. She left me alone. Another patient, who was male and obviously confused, kept wandering through the gap in the curtains, and I could hear a nurse telling him firmly to leave that area and go back to his own bed. For goodness' sake, this was a night I would never ever forget. I vowed that if I ever got to that stage in my life then I WOULD throw myself off the Humber Bridge. I really wasn't sure if I was participating in an actual television medical drama or a comedy scene at that precise point. It was surreal and too traumatic to laugh or even cry.

Sheila was cold to touch, so I guessed that the phone call was made when she had already died. I was asked by a nurse to remove her jewellery; her rings and a gold watch that Andrew had bought her many years ago – her favourite watch. I was handed her clothes in a hospital carrier bag, and that was it. The end. I leant over and kissed her on her right cheek, hugged her frail, tiny body tightly, said I was sorry and that I always loved her. Then I walked away crying, trying to hold onto her carrier bag of clothes and also trying to hold onto my imminent sobbing until I got back to the privacy of my car in the hospital car park. Merry Fucking Christmas 2021, everyone.

My emotional state was made even worse as I knew that Sheila was the nearest person I had to a proper mother. SHE was the only one who said she loved me as a daughter. After all, I loved and cared for her only son. She was grateful, and I knew that. I knew she was a bit of a nag at times, but deep down I still loved her. I put a lot of her nagging down to her age. It was understandable. She used to say to me, 'There's only me and thee now, lass. We have to look after one another,' and I used to nod, holding back tears as I knew she was right, now that Andrew had gone. I was convinced that the shock and trauma of Andrew's sudden death helped her on the way to her own. I felt like dying most days but had to carry on. I even asked myself why I actually kept on going. It would be easier to just give up and give in.

I, unfortunately, had to keep on working, as boring and mundane as work was, as it paid the bills. I had learnt to be a good actress – laughing and joking with customers on the phone at work, but when the phone was off, I went back into my own private world. I didn't especially want to talk to anyone. I wanted to be left alone to mentally comprehend and understand the last few emotional months of trauma and grief.

Everything had now gone, all my future hopes and dreams, along with my sanity and any principles I used to have. I shouldn't be having one-night stands, or even seeing men that were 'attached' to others, and not giving a shit. There again, in my defence, THEY had put themselves onto dating apps. If it wasn't me, it would be someone else they would be shagging. I also could be just one of the many women they were shagging! Who knew? I didn't. I now had blurred lines in so many areas of my life, whereas at one time it would have been either wrong or right, black or white. Everything was now suddenly mixed into one big pot of 'anything goes, fuck it, just do it'.

Sheila passing away made me think more about mortality; it had hit me hard. Her and Andrew were close, too close at times, and couldn't live without each other. What else could I bloody cope with? Andrew would have wanted me to look after his mother, putting his trust in me, and now look at it. Both had died within seven months of each other. Guilt is a terrible emotion, nearly as bad as grief. Guilt that I couldn't save Andrew; and guilt that Sheila died without me seeing her and being there for her, due to COVID restrictions.

My emotions felt surreal, as if I was driving a car, head-on at a brick wall, like a crash test dummy. Would the impact kill me, or would I survive? I didn't really care anymore. I was becoming out of control in so many ways in my life now, and had seriously had enough. I certainly couldn't think straight and logically like I used to.

I had been given a medical fit note by my doctor's surgery after Andrew's death, for a few weeks, and just expected to go back to work and carry on with my life as if nothing had changed. No follow-up or recommendation to see a counsellor; I was just expected to carry on regardless. I didn't even see the doctor; I couldn't get an appointment, so certainly wouldn't bother after Sheila died as there seemed no point. People were still asking me questions such as – 'Will you sell your house?', 'Why don't you downsize?' Well, what did it matter? I would still be alone whether I stayed in my marital house or sold it to downsize. Such ridiculous questions that I had no patience with. It was too early for any decisions to be made. Only my close friends understood. Moving house or location didn't matter – I would be alone whether I moved or not. Didn't people realise that?

I wasn't sure what I wanted anymore, just that I wanted to be left alone. I needed some respite but also some fun. Yes, I had been out with married men. It was easier as they would just go back to their wives and nothing more would be said. It became an addiction, all the highs and lows of having an affair, this time controlled entirely by me. I used to say in my head that if their wives spent more time shagging than nagging, then their men wouldn't look elsewhere. But maybe that was because I never nagged at anyone, even in my marriage. Andrew wasn't a possession or a child; why would I nag? Maybe I was just too independent, businesslike and strong-willed for most men. Only Andrew understood and gave me as much freedom as I wanted. Our pact was never to stray, and we both stuck by that rule; that was the only rule we had. I knew I had too much to lose by having an affair.

My mind wandered – Andrew had unfairly been publicly humiliated many times. He went on *Come Dine With Me* when we first met. The other contestants called him boring. He was mortified. What they didn't know was that he was MY boring boyfriend. MY faithful, reliable, dependable bore. Who never ever let me down. Who laughed and cried with me, who cared for and loved me. Let them think he was a bore; he was as geeky and as boring as I was at times.

Only Andrew had kept me level-headed and grounded over the past years, but now he had gone, the ground was quickly slipping from beneath me. I certainly wasn't grounded anymore; I was at ground zero.

CHAPTER 11

DRINKING FROM THE BOTTLE

We had our works annual Christmas party. My employer was generous and always paid for a meal, drinks and sometimes a hotel room overnight in Leeds for all employees. This year, he was paying for the full lot. Bloody fantastic! I would be making the most of it; I needed some enjoyment after the last traumatic week or so.

I was now sorting out yet another funeral, along with the added stress of trying to empty Sheila's flat, which was like Dr Who's TARDIS. Her never-ending possessions, rammed into cupboards and drawers, were now coming out of her flat straight into my estate car to be brought back to my house. My own house was now beginning to resemble a hoarders' paradise for pensioners, and I bloody hated it. It actually now looked like Sheila's flat, and it depressed me. I was too ill after my operation to even sort it out, and boxes were now piled everywhere, along with suitcases full of her clothes and possessions. It drove me insane as I had only just managed to sort out my own house. This, along with continual phone calls, drove me bloody crazy. Ringing the hospital to sort out the death certificate, cancelling bank accounts, cancelling her rent, and all the usual endless aftermath of paperwork and legal stuff. I could have possibly set up my own business in administrating funeral arrangements and banking matters. I seemed to be on a constant treadmill of work, and then sorting out other people's crap, alone. It was now becoming too overwhelming.

My attention span was now very short, and I got bored easily. I was now bored at the works Christmas party in the posh spa hotel; it seemed never-ending and time was going so slowly. I had been there nearly two hours and had eaten my Christmas meal and tried to make small talk above the noise of the music in the background. I had drunk most of the free bottles of beer that were on the table in a massive beer bucket full of ice, alternated it with some white wine, and was now drunk, but I didn't care.

Our plates were cleared away and the disco started up once again. I must be the only person that hates fucking Motown music, and I sighed a drunken sigh when some of the girls from work were laughing in excitement and getting up to dance. The horrendous music blasted out of the speakers. This was seriously enough to tip me over the edge; my false smile had now gone and I was becoming impatient. Now the music turned to ABBA and *Dancing Queen*. For goodness' sake! This year, I was definitely out of patience with it all, and looking more for a fight or a good fuck than a friggin' girly dance.

I staggered across the large room, accidentally knocking into tables and chairs as I went, to find the ladies' toilets. Almost falling off the toilet seat sideways when I sat down to have a wee. I knew this was not a good sign and it meant I was too drunk, too soon. I'd forgotten about the alcoholic drinks I had drunk in my hotel room, even before I had come downstairs for this so-called Christmas meal. I staggered out of the toilets and had to walk near the bar area to get back into the main room again. I had drunk enough beer and foolishly decided that I would order a Bacardi and Coke at the bar. I just handed my bank card to the person serving behind the bar, as I couldn't even see straight to pay. He had to swipe my card for me; I was incapable. My body was swaying now, and I almost felt seasick, especially in my sparkly black high heels.

There was a young bloke near the bar who I singled out, and we got chatting. I will use that word 'chatting' very loosely as I think I was slurring my words rather than speaking coherently. 'Come to my room, I have brought some champagne with me,' I drunkenly slurred. We swapped mobile numbers out of courtesy and had a laugh and a joke. The next thing I remember was both of us getting into the hotel lift, on the way to the top floor where my bedroom was.

I opened the champagne from the fridge in my room and told him to wait whilst I got showered. Goodness knows why I had this idea of getting into a shower, as I was so drunk that I had to hold onto the tiled walls of the shower to stop myself falling over. But I wasn't going to let this opportunity pass me by. *Dancing Queen*, or a fuck? There was no competition really. I came out of the shower and attempted to dry myself with one of the hotel's nice soft white fluffy towels but gave up and just lay on my back on the bed, naked, and let him do the work. The room was now spinning at a rapid speed.

I fell asleep, a very deep drunken sleep. He must have left my room and gone back to his own room. I was woken by text messages beeping on my mobile phone at 2am. It was him, texting me his room number and asking me to come over for round number two. Well, I couldn't even remember round number one! It must have been good, I suppose; otherwise, he wouldn't have messaged me. Who knows? I certainly didn't. I had sobered up a bit after a couple of hours' sleep, probably snoring as I do when I have had a lot to drink. I even wake myself up with my own snoring as it is so loud. Maybe that was why he left my room. Who knows? I eventually found my lace panties, which had been randomly thrown into a corner of my room, found a white towelling hotel dressing gown from inside the wardrobe, grabbed my room key and trotted across the corridor. Praying in my head that no one from work would see me, as I couldn't cope with any questions, and I certainly had no plausible answers.

I knocked on his door and he let me into the room. We both laughed. I said that obviously once wasn't enough, and he agreed. He dived under the duvet in his large hotel bed, and I joined him. He began vaping and watching his laptop at the side of the bed; some cricket match was streaming live from Australia. He had stuffed a sock into the smoke detector of the hotel room and I laughed about that, telling him he was very naughty and shouldn't be vaping. This was one unreal night; I wasn't sure if I was dreaming – I wasn't.

The hotel rooms were also used for business, and each room had a massive work desk with a swivel chair. We got out of bed and acted out role play, pretending to be in an office at work, me dragging the swivel chair out from under the desk and trying to have sex whilst sat on the chair. My drunken plans never work, and the chair moved too quickly across the room on its castors and went crashing loudly into the large wooden desk, then smashed noisily into the large radiator. Bloody hell, the whole of the hotel would be awake by now! We both gave up with that idea and got into the bed instead, the safer option for both of us. Who cared that he was due to get married in a few months' time? I didn't. I would show him a good time before he was married, as I could guarantee that when he WAS married then the sex would almost stop. Hmm, there were some things that I DID like about Christmas after all, and it certainly wasn't *Dancing Queen.*

CHAPTER 12

OH CUM, ALL YE UNFAITHFUL

It was nearly the end of this traumatic year. Yet life went on and I was still carrying on with the practical things in life. Starting with the cars; they needed to get through their MOTs. Andrew used to go to his friend who had a garage down in Leicester, but after that expensive bill in May, left for me to pay for the Range Rover repairs and the Volvo, I certainly wasn't going to that garage again – ever. I booked the cars into a local garage instead. Having to drop one car off and walk home, then driving the other one there. It was okay; I didn't mind walking. Although it was freezing cold in December, it gave me time to think, even though that could be dangerous sometimes.

Mechanic Boy at the garage recognised me from bringing the Range Rover in for a repair a few months previous, before I sold it. That car was a bloody burden. I dropped off both cars as we made small talk. I said I would walk back to the garage after work at 5pm to collect both the cars after they had passed their MOTs.

I went back at 5pm and Mechanic Boy was still repairing one of the cars. I raised my eyebrows and tutted as he told me he had difficulty removing the locking nuts on the wheels, like it was a big deal. I didn't have time for any further small talk. I abruptly asked how long he would be. He replied, 'Not long.' I paid for both cars and drove the first one home and would return for the other one an hour later. Nothing else was said except a polite thank-you and goodbye.

That night, I was at home doing paperwork when I received a random text message from Mechanic Boy. *I hope the cars are okay?* And more messages: *You know where I am if you need anything ... What are you doing for Christmas?* Well, I didn't need anything, as I had car breakdown cover anyway. I was doing bugger all for Christmas, which was none of his business anyway. I thought it was a bit random but noticed his full name was on the MOT certificate, so I looked on

Facebook to see if he was on there, and also his status. His profile was open to all, and he WAS there, as large as life, with his profile picture showing him with his arm around a woman. Looking further at his photos, he also had children. For goodness' sake, he was a family man.

I quickly sent him a text message back: *I am confused. It looks like you have a girlfriend or wife, and children.*

He replied blatantly, *Oh yeah, so what?* I asked him if he messaged other women who took their cars to the garage for repairs or an MOT. He admitted he did. I sent a jokey message back saying it was just like his personal 'garage Tinder'. But secretly I was annoyed. How dare he message me on my own private mobile number and then flirt? He needed to be taught a lesson. I felt uneasy about the whole thing. His partner/wife was a lot bigger than me in size and would certainly win in a fight, but she was definitely welcome to him. He was too sleazy for me. But I kept him on the back burner; after all, he would be useful if my cars needed repairing. He could be my own personal mechanic, at MY beck and call.

A few nights later, I was out jogging, determined to lose weight after my operation. It was Christmas Eve, and the weather was still mild but fresh. My phone bleeped with a text message from Mechanic Boy. *I'm in the local park walking the dog. Meet me.* I couldn't resist; I knew it was wrong, but it was also enticing. I jogged into the park and met him, and we ended up snogging and groping in the dark in the local park, out of sight of any CCTV cameras. It was as if I was about seventeen years old again. We hid away from anyone. He had tied the dog's lead to a post nearby and it was now watching us and whimpering for attention; a bit off-putting, but I carried on regardless, not caring. After all, I was now in control; he had broken his vows. I hadn't. I was single and could do what the hell I liked.

I woke up on Christmas Day, obviously in bed alone. It was a strange feeling as there was no one next to me to hug and say, 'Merry Christmas, I love you' to. I tried not to feel guilty about the previous night in the park – Mechanic Boy was a distraction, nothing else. The only good thing about today was that I didn't have to go to work. In fact, I didn't even have to get out of bed. I needed a bloody good rest after the last few weeks.

I had already decided to log onto the chatlines to take calls. After all, it was a bank holiday, and I would increase my prices per minute to reflect that. I guessed I would get more clients the next day, on Boxing Day. Whilst the wives or partners were queuing outside in the freezing cold, at the Boxing Day sales, usually outside NEXT. I could almost guarantee the men would be sighing with relief, and also wanting relief, when Christmas Day was over. All the false festivities and family dramas, the stress of sitting with family members they didn't even like and hadn't seen since the previous Christmas, and certainly wouldn't see again until the next Christmas. The hassle of cooking a Christmas dinner, opening presents that they didn't want, or even like. The list of stresses went on and on at Christmas. I wasn't being cynical, just truthful.

'Anything for a quiet life,' the married men used to tell me. 'I have to keep her indoors happy or my life won't be worth living.' I used to pretend to agree with them but would secretly think to myself, *Thank fuck I don't have to put up with that anymore.* So, I couldn't really complain about Christmas. After all, I had it easy compared to some families and could do what the heck I wanted, when I wanted and with whomever I wanted.

Clients that were bored rang me on the chatlines late Christmas morning. I repeated constantly the usual chit-chat and flirty talk about pulling their Christmas cracker and asking them if they had been a good boy over the past year, talking at them like they were small naughty children. They seemed to love it when I mentioned Santa's sack, roast chestnuts and all the innuendos that went with the festive season. I was seriously getting too good at this and even amazed myself sometimes with my flirty and comedic talk. It was suddenly as if I was performing a personalised Christmas comedy gig on the phone to them, or even a pantomime. I was really getting into this seasonal acting and comedy sketches a bit too much, and I even made myself laugh at my own innuendos. I watched the money accumulate over the day. After all, I had nothing else worthwhile to do. Whilst I was on the phone, at least I wasn't sobbing, so that was a positive.

One client, Jason, rang me; he had a soft southern accent. I had to keep him talking as I was now charging £1 a minute for a bank holiday 'special'. 'Time is money', as I was told in private industry, along with, 'We always aim to give Best Value'. Yeah, how right they were. This was MY time and MY money. Jason told me he had just put his defrosted turkey in the oven to cook and was waiting for his parents to come round to his house for Christmas dinner but needed 'relief' before he saw his parents as he was stressed. All I could think was *for goodness' sake!* and I raised my eyebrows – well, the best I could after having Botox on my forehead. At least he was honest, and I knew he needed to cum before his Christmas turkey would be cooked. I ended up asking him how big the turkey was and how long it had already been in the oven. This was now turning into a blooming Fanny Craddock cookery lesson, not a sexy chatline! I just hoped his parents wouldn't arrive early at his house and catch him with his phone in one hand, his cock in the other and the turkey burning in the oven! I did laugh to myself with a vision of this in my head ... I was either now seriously mentally deranged or just past caring. I couldn't work out which. But it was comedy gold whichever way you looked at it.

How my life had changed in just a few months. Yes, this was certainly a different Christmas.

My wedding day to Andrew was the best day of my life. His death was the worst day of my life.

My childhood friends helped and supported me through my breakdowns and my craziest times.

I invited my ex-boyfriend Garry back into my life – to say goodbye

A photograph from my chatlines webpage. I needed money so promoted myself as a MILF and a tart.

PART TWO
2022

CHAPTER 1 – TIME TO SAY GOODBYE 61
CHAPTER 2 – FREE FALLIN' 66
CHAPTER 3 – AIRPORT 70
CHAPTER 4 – OPPORTUNITIES (LET'S MAKE LOTS OF MONEY) 75
CHAPTER 5 – ON THE FLOOR 80
CHAPTER 6 – COLD AS ICE 85
CHAPTER 7 – ONE STEP BEYOND 88
CHAPTER 8 – SULTANS OF SWING 93
CHAPTER 9 – FADE TO GREY 99
CHAPTER 10 – ERASE/REWIND 103
CHAPTER 11 – DRIVER'S SEAT 106
CHAPTER 12 – HUNGRY LIKE THE WOLF 111
CHAPTER 13 – BLUE MONDAY 113
CHAPTER 14 – ASHES TO ASHES 117
CHAPTER 15 – SWING WHEN YOU'RE WINNING 121
CHAPTER 16 – LEARNING TO FLY (BUT I AIN'T GOT WINGS) ..125
CHAPTER 17 – OUT OF MY DEPTH 129
CHAPTER 18 – CURIOSITY KILLED THE CAT 134
CHAPTER 19 – WALK ON THE WILD SIDE 141
CHAPTER 20 – WANK HOLIDAY WEEKEND 145
CHAPTER 21 – SUICIDE BLONDE 150

CHAPTER 1

TIME TO SAY GOODBYE

Time to Say Goodbye by Andrea Bocelli and Sarah Brightman – one of Andrew's favourite pieces of music whenever we went to the Bellagio Hotel and fountains in Las Vegas. Now seemingly appropriate, and now sadly, my time to say goodbye in 2021, to them both, forever.

It was January 2022 and I would have loved to say 'Happy New Year' but knew there would be nothing happy about it. It was just another traumatic day. I had spent a miserable, depressive Christmas time and New Year's Day – alone, by my own choice. I tried to act cheerful, but it was hard and I was still in shock. I had endured seven months of different and strange experiences, and not all positive ones. How could I even justify or explain my recent stupidity and actions? I couldn't.

The Christmas carol *The Twelve Days of Christmas* was nothing compared to my own last few days before Christmas. I had my own version ending in: five mental breakdowns, four drunken shags, three days on the chatlines, two random fumbles and a blow job in the local park. That was hardly a traditional Christmas. It was certainly different, to say the least, but definitely not traditional. I suppose not many people could say that was how they celebrated their Christmas – but I could. I had no shame.

I kept quiet. If people asked me if I had a good Christmas, I would say, 'Oh yes, but it was very quiet.' Then I would get the look of sympathy and words of comfort such as, 'Yes, I am so sorry, it can't have been easy for you.' I could hardly tell anyone the truth; they would be shocked by my drunken, irrational, now compulsive sexual and sleazy behaviour.

I still had to arrange and finalise Sheila's funeral. I had already spoken to the vicar on the phone and we had a video chat online, where I expressed my wish for the funeral to be a quiet ceremony. I thanked (sarcastically) the undertaker for sending me an email actually on Christmas Day – just to remind me of her imminent funeral in January. As if I could even forget that! Hadn't I had enough upset and trauma without their triggering reminders? I took it with a pinch of salt as I was now past caring about everything. It was probably just an automated email – that just happened to be sent on Christmas Day!

I still had Sheila's 'treasured possessions' to sell. The truth was that they were almost worthless in these modern times. I knew this for a fact as she had been to the *Antiques Roadshow* when it was visiting and recording at Beverley Minster a few years previous. Knowing her, she was probably first in the queue with her trolley load of items – twenty-seven in all. The whole lot valued at maximum £3,000. I personally think they may have overestimated the value, just to keep her quiet. She thought she was sitting on a fortune. Well, unfortunately for her, and now me, she wasn't.

I sold all her white goods on the internet. Then hired a stall for £50 at a local antiques fair for the rest of her aged possessions to be sold. I was lucky to break even that day. I was bored shitless. Standing behind my hired stall full of tapestries, old teapots, horse brasses, ornaments and old decorative plates with pictures of the royal family on them. Funnily enough, the decorative plate that had a picture of Prince Andrew and Sarah Ferguson on it drew most attention and was a talking point for all. All these things on the stall were, unfortunately, only fit for the dustbin and I now realised this. What a waste of a day.

I had to listen to all sorts of ridiculous conversations from various people, one customer even accusing me of fiddling my income tax by having a stall, as I would only accept cash, not card payments. She was almost stabbing her finger at me for not having a card reader. I just laughed in her face and said I DID pay my tax, thank you very much, and worked full time, and would be lucky to make even £20 from this shambolic shitshow. I replied that if she wanted to report me to the tax office to please go ahead. That soon shut her up! It was certainly an eye-opener in Doncaster that day. Never again. I learnt to keep quiet behind that stall before I flipped my lid to some other argumentative customer. Who the fuck did they think they were? They all tested my patience.

I was now bored, cold and fed up. I couldn't wait to leave and go home. Unfortunately, my car had just as much vintage and old crappy stuff loaded into it going home as it did when it bloody arrived there. At home, I sorted items into bundles – the local refuse tip and charity shops. I hadn't time for it all, as I was busy and still working. I had learnt and mastered one thing that day, which was how to show that I had a FOF – a 'Fuck-Off Face'. A look I could give to anyone when they were annoying me, and they seemed to know to either shut up or just walk away. Good, that worked well then. Yes, this whole day had been a total waste of a day, and I was more annoyed with myself for thinking I could make a profit. Or even sell the items for them to be recycled. I could have spent the day on the chatlines instead, and made a lot of money from the comfort of my own home sat in front of the television still in my pyjamas. Never mind – you live and learn, and I was a bloody quick learner nowadays.

The funeral for Sheila was held at Beverley Minster in January 2022. My friend Caroline came with me for support, as did one of Andrew's best friends from London and his girlfriend. For which I will be eternally grateful, as they knew I was bloody done with it all and on the verge of a nervous breakdown.

I told the undertaker that I wanted this day to be over with as quickly as possible as I had had enough trauma over the last few months. I was out of everything – tears, conversation, patience and money. You name it – I was bloody out of it. I was physically and mentally drained, more than people would ever know. I became an observer in conversations, not a participant like I used to be. It was too much effort to even hold a conversation. To be honest, I could have just stayed in bed all day and all night, and it wouldn't even have bothered me. I was still physically weak, tired and emotional after my operation but had to carry on. I asked myself in my mind, *WHAT was I carrying on for, and WHO was I carrying on for?* The answer to that was – only for my friends. I knew they would be devastated if I did something stupid.

I had arranged for the hearse to come to Sheila's flat first, as it was near the Minster, as I, somewhat incorrectly, presumed that her remaining family would meet the hearse at her flat. I had kept her settee, chairs and a kettle for hot drinks in the flat deliberately for this purpose. I shouldn't have presumed. I was at that flat waiting that morning – alone. Let's just say I was disappointed. I was past being angry. After all, it wasn't MY family. I had already disowned mine and was now grateful for the peace and quiet without them. I was used to being alone now, so this day was no different really.

The hearse driver picked up on my prominent Hull accent and smiled at me. He asked where I lived in Hull. We made a bit of small talk about moving out of Hull. He didn't know that only a few months previous I was a passenger in another funeral car, outside my own house, following my husband's coffin. Life seemed so unfair – to lose my beloved husband and then his mother within a few months. I glanced at the hearse driver and thought he looked like the Fat Controller from the *Thomas the Tank Engine* television series all those years ago, when my son used to watch it in the 1990s. My mind began to wander. Yes, those faraway, good old days when I had my son and love. Now look at it. A horrendous divorce, I'd lost my son and had now lost my husband and my fucking mind. I stifled a sarcastic, nonchalant smile and climbed into the back of the large black Mercedes funeral car that was now following the hearse.

Unfortunately, as I put my foot into the back of the car to sit down, I managed to accidently break the plastic foot plate off the car with my high-heeled boots. I laughed about it – I was just so bloody clumsy. I handed the broken pieces to the driver, with the question, 'These are yours, I believe?'

'What the heck have you done?' he asked.

'Sorry, I have accidently broken this off your car. Please charge it to the family, they'll pay,' and I laughed about it. I think I had actually forgotten how to laugh.

After the funeral at Beverley Minster, Sheila's close family eventually got into the car, and we set off to go to the cemetery, literally in a deathly silence. I certainly had nothing to say to anyone anymore.

It was a freezing cold, damp and miserable day. The gravediggers had overlapped the artificial grass around the grave. Sheila had a shared plot with her husband, and there was mud around the grave that had been covered up. Unfortunately, someone from her family had stumbled and managed to move the artificial grass with their great big clodhopper shoes, so it was all ridged up. I then managed to trip over the grass, and my high heel stuck in the mud and the artificial tufts of grass. The Fat Controller man was watching me and put his hands out as if to catch me before I almost fell into the grave. It was like a comedy scene, but it wasn't funny; it was a bloody tragedy.

Sadly, it was the first time I had ever been grateful for Andrew dying before his mother, as he wouldn't have been able to cope with the stress and grief of his mother's funeral. I knew his mother's health had declined rapidly since his death. I did genuinely feel sorry for her, as Andrew was her whole life – as he was mine. She absolutely doted on him. I will never forget going to her flat and breaking the news to her that Andrew had died during the night. She had thought I was going to tell her that he had been admitted to hospital, as he'd been unwell for a while. How I even managed to drive to Beverley that morning to tell her, sobbing to myself in my car, is beyond me. Grief can have such an effect on those left behind, as I would find out even more over the next few months.

CHAPTER 2

FREE FALLIN'

I went off the fucking rails, big time. Even more than the previous month. If that was even possible. My house didn't just need a new front door; it needed a bloody turnstile, with men literally coming and going. I may as well have handed out wristbands, like on all-inclusive holidays in 5-star hotels. All inclusive? Half board? Just a blow job? Just a wank? Full sex? Who knew anymore? I certainly didn't.

I am not usually a heavy drinker – I can hold my drink well – but I made sure I had a few drinks each night to get me through. I certainly wasn't an alcoholic, but alcohol helped blot out the mental and tragic pain I was feeling of being alone and coping with grief. I needed a break from everything. Work was causing me stress beyond belief, the continual helpdesk calls and company statistics, along with performance reviews – Jeeeez ... just give me a bloody break. Two major deaths and a tumour removed – and I was expected to come back to work laughing and joking, or 'We would like the old Helen back,' as one person said. Well, it was never fucking going to happen – I told them that outright. They weren't impressed.

I could work on autopilot most of the time and be sociable; I was quickly learning to be a good actress, although when at work by 10am, I was crying large hot tears into my cup of coffee. I had to have regular short breaks to have a good 5-minute sob to myself. Forget using normal tissues; they were far too flimsy for my large tears. I had now progressed on to thick kitchen roll and industrial blue roll, much more absorbent and practical for my needs. Why had no one invented large super-sized absorbent tissues especially for grief? Was it because no one cried as much as I did? Was I the only one? Possibly. Forget a small bedroom bin to dispose of the wet, soggy kitchen roll, this was now on an industrial scale. Blue roll, kitchen roll and a large orange builder's bucket from B&Q in the corner of my bedroom for their disposal. My bedroom was now the sobbing room.

Every working day I eagerly counted down the hours until 4pm, when I could log off work. Then I could go up to my bedroom, which used to be the marital bedroom, and cry to myself for a few hours. I needed time to comprehend all this. It was as if I had to analyse and dissect the last few months. I didn't know why. I couldn't turn the clock back. What had happened, HAD happened.

I imagined I was falling through a broken handrail, falling downwards, then randomly falling through broken ice, plunging down and not knowing if I would survive the icy water and come back up to the surface for breath. Strange feelings, and now I was having nightmares that seemed so real, so real that I would wake up with my heart racing and a sore throat, possibly from screaming in my sleep. I now daren't sleep. I was shattered. This was worse than *Nightmare on Elm Street*, when you go to sleep and your nightmares become reality. That was one of my favourite horror films many years ago. Unfortunately, it was now MY bloody reality. Andrew would never watch my horror films as they scared him shitless; now I was scaring myself shitless just by going to sleep. There was no escape. Just like with Freddy Krueger and the parody 'One, two, Freddy's coming for you'. I now knew that feeling only too well as now I daren't even close my eyes.

I needed another distraction, another fix. I needed sex, as now, to me, it was cheaper than alcohol, if that is any consolation. I now just used men, as they used me. I had no emotion, just fuck them and tell them to fuck off. They had served their purpose. A bit like my ladies' disposable shaver that I used for my legs – use once and then discard. Thrown straight into the waste bin and immediately forgotten about. Yeah – men were like disposable ladies' shavers to me. Tossed off and tossed away. I wasn't sure if this was now a revenge tactic by me, a bit like on one of my favourite films, *I Spit on Your Grave*. Getting revenge on men. Who knew? I certainly didn't, but I knew WHY I would do it, from how I was treated in my previous marriage and relationships. They had all caused me resentment and now revenge. I took no prisoners in my life.

Tinder was beckoning me again. I should have known better, and I DID know better. The compulsion was too strong and I logged on. Danny from Leeds had such a beautiful body on his profile picture. He was only thirty-nine years old; I was almost twenty years older. He had tanned or naturally dark skin, was slim and had a six-pack. He was 'sex on legs'. I invited him to come and see me one night. He looked Turkish with his dark hair and rugged looks. I certainly wasn't going to ask him his nationality or ethnicity; that was irrelevant. I just wanted him in my bed. Well, in the spare bedroom anyway. Rules are rules in my house, and no one was allowed into my own bedroom, now the sobbing room, or into the marital bed. It was sacred, and as much as I had no morals anymore, I had to have some respect. Plus, it was STILL bloody broken!

I was shameless, and certainly not blameless. Danny was certainly 'sex on legs' and we had mind- blowing sex. Although he was having a drag of his e-cigarette between sessions. Oh well, as long as it didn't set the smoke detectors off in the house, I didn't care. I had learnt to be more accepting of people and their quirks or habits. Our 'meet-ups' kept going for seven months or so; we finally just drifted apart. Danny wasn't one of the 'disposable' ones in my life; he was soft and sweet and literally melted my heart when he softly kissed me. He had a thing about even numbers; his favourite was the number four. In other words, we had good sex four times in a row. He was crazy for it, and so was I. Sometimes, it's good to be shameless, I laughed to myself. I just didn't care.

Tom was yet another hook-up from Tinder. He lived locally but daren't come round to see me. So why was he on Tinder? I asked him that and he said he didn't know but said he had affairs before. I wasn't sure if I believed him; maybe he was full of bullshit. It took him months to summon up the courage to see me. He was apparently married, as are most of the men who are on Tinder. I asked what his wife didn't do to him that he wanted me to do ... he said he wanted me to act like a dominatrix and have power over him. Well, the way I felt about life, men and the future, that was bloody easy. I could easily shout, swear and certainly be demanding, and get it out of my system. Every other word that came out of my mouth now was a swear word anyway. It was like my own second language.

'Just come round and I will see what I can do,' I sighed loudly on the phone at him. It was now as if I was running a bloody brothel. Twenty minutes later, he came round in his builder's van. Not exactly very flipping discreet. I never saw him again, and I'm not bothered. But at least if he died tomorrow, he would hopefully die happy, or happier. I just didn't care anymore. No one would ever find out unless he told them – and more fool him if he did. My turnstile was certainly getting some use this month.

CHAPTER 3

AIRPORT

Loy's profile showed up randomly on one of my Tinder searches. Looking at his profile photo, he was really attractive, although there was something weird about the angle of the photo, like it had been cropped and photoshopped. His photo just happened to be taken in front of a commercial aeroplane, and he was wearing a pilot's uniform. I zoomed in; there was the logo for Lufthansa airline in the background. I was left wondering if he was German. But Lufthansa didn't fly from our local airports. So how did his profile appear in my local search area? All this should have given me red flags to stay away. Not the nationality – but the actual photos, which looked unnatural. I was intrigued. Was he for real? If so, why was he single? Sometimes, curiosity got the better of me. I should really know better and, at my age, just stay well away and ignore it. Move on. Walk away. Unfortunately, I couldn't.

Loy messaged me on Tinder with some personal information. I replied briefly, as I knew something wasn't quite right with this scenario. But I felt compelled to continue. He told me in his messages that he was a single parent and had a small child who lived with a nanny abroad, but he was determined to bring her over to the UK to live with him. Additionally, if we all got on, then we could all live together. I was puzzled – this bloke, whom I didn't even know, was now talking about ME living with him and his child. What the hell? He said he wanted to talk away from Tinder messages, and more privately, on a separate app – Google Hangouts. I said okay and installed the app. It was no great loss to me. I could just uninstall the app and that would be it; he wouldn't be able to contact me again.

Unbeknown to me, he could actually ring me from bloody Google Hangouts! Shit! I didn't know that as I had never used it before. The first time he rang was when I was shopping in the local Tesco supermarket early one Saturday morning. I felt I had to answer the call as my mobile phone was ringing a strange ringtone, very loudly, in my jacket pocket. I answered and quickly walked back to my car for a more private conversation. I was embarrassed and annoyed at the same time.

I had never even spoken to him before. I certainly never wanted him to randomly call me. As I answered, he was acting like a bloody lovestruck teenager in the way he was talking childish gibberish and flirting. I hate men that flirt in that way; it's such a turn-off. I told him that his accent sounded almost Jamaican, yet he had told me he was half Norwegian in his messages, so I was a bit surprised. According to him, he had picked up an American and mixed Jamaican accent as he flew regularly to the United States and his deceased wife was American. Therefore, he must have picked up some of her accent too. 'Oh, okay,' I said, as I wasn't really bothered about him or his accent. 'I had better go and finish my shopping and get back home.' I was bored of him already and his so-called half-truths. He was prattling on for ages and coming on too strong. Asking personal questions such as what car I drove, and did I have a house or a flat? I avoided answering them truthfully, the nosy sod. Luckily, on Tinder I had given a false name and area of where I lived, so he had no chance of tracing me. He seemed like bloody hard work, and totally extreme in his questioning, mannerisms and attitude.

The conversations and text messages continued over the next few weeks on Google Hangouts. If I ignored his calls as I was working or busy, I would then receive half a dozen texts all at once, asking if I was all right, continually pestering me, sending stupid flower emojis and love hearts. I really should have closed down the conversation there and then, but something inside me felt compelled to continue it, just to see how far he would go. I was busy and didn't have time for distractions like this, but I knew he was full of lies and I was intrigued. I had already sent him abrupt, if not almost aggressive, messages, such as *I – AM – BUSY – AT – WORK!* but still he persisted and didn't seem to take the bloody hint.

In fact, he had sent a pathetic message back: *Aww, don't you want to speak to me, honey? I miss you.*

I replied *NO*. I couldn't have been any bloody clearer. But still he continued his game of cat and mouse. Unfortunately, I was the mouse.

One day, he suddenly messaged me and said he had to travel to an oil rig off Aberdeen for some staff training. He was flying the helicopter with other staff on board, for a safety training session. Okay, that was feasible, I suppose, even though he was supposed to be a commercial airline pilot for a German airline! I was hoping he would just piss off onto the oil rig, if it was true. Then I would have a week or so free from his ridiculous text messages and him annoying me by calling at all hours. My phone and iPad were now on constant silent mode so I didn't have to listen to it ringing and him wittering on, along with his text messages continually pinging.

He seemed to want to tell me every detail. *I'm just packing my suitcase, princess,* he messaged me. I ignored his message and his stupid suitcase photograph that he sent. A few days later, he sent me a picture of the oil rig, allegedly in Aberdeen. Apparently, he had only just got there. Well, that was a long flight then of three days! The picture was taken from a boat near the oil rig, with a helicopter in mid-air waiting to land on the helipad. He put in the text with the photo (thinking he was clever), *This is our dinner arriving on the oil rig via helicopter.*

I replied sarcastically, *Well, where is YOUR helicopter then? As you cannot get two helicopters on that helipad at the same time. And why are you on a boat in the sea, where are you? I am so confused …* I sniggered to myself as I sent the message. I seriously didn't have time for this shit.

He was an idiot. He had obviously got a photo of a random oil rig from the internet. I had already caught him out. His oil rig photograph had a number on its side; I had googled it. He said he was off the coast of Aberdeen. This was, not surprisingly, untrue, as the oil rig photo he sent was of one based offshore in Saudi Arabia. *You can't kid me, babe,*

I thought. This was giving me more and more ammunition daily. It was becoming a daily challenge, and I really should have told him to fuck off there and then and just uninstalled the app. But I strangely felt the need to continue, just to see what he was building up to. This was going to be sooooo much fun to catch him out at every chance. How dare he lie to me and waste my time. I would now waste HIS time.

The next time he rang, he asked what time it was where I was. I said it was the same time as it was where HE was in Scotland. He said he was confused. I told him that the time zone in Scotland was the same as England. He was just so dopey. At least he could have done his research from Jamaica, Africa, America or wherever he was based. Suddenly there was a long pause on the phone.

He ignored my response about the time zone and changed the subject. Now he was waffling on with a sob story that before he set off on his journey to the oil rig, his credit card had been stolen and therefore stopped by the bank, and now he was short of money. I replied, 'Well, there is nothing to spend money on at the oil rig, is there? Also, the bank will re-issue you with a new credit card immediately. It will be on your doormat when you return home, so there's really no need to worry.' I noticed that that conversation was cut short instantly. I laughed to myself, now guessing that he was building up to asking for money.

The next time Loy rang, I could hear constant chattering in the background. 'Oh, I am in the staff quarters,' he said, 'it is very noisy, the staff are so excited with the training on the rigs today. It went well.'

'Oh good,' I replied, not that bothered. The next thing I heard was a crashing noise, car horns honking noisily and people shouting and swearing. 'Ooh, that sounds like cars I can hear. It almost sounds like a car crash, you know, like an accident,' I said, 'but I must be hearing things, as I know you are obviously on the rigs.' There was no reply, but I could suddenly hear heavy footsteps and then doors or windows slamming shut. Obviously, he was in a room (on dry land!) with the windows open and there was a traffic jam outside, possibly resulting in an accident. I knew he wasn't really on the rigs, but he genuinely thought I believed him and would fall for his charm, smarm and constant lies.

His flirty patter was relentless, and he continued it in text messages with phrases such as: *You are my beautiful queen ... I love you so much ... Babe, you must eat or you will be ill ... You need to rest, you've done a lot today.* Then more emojis of love hearts and bunches of roses. It was total message overload, trying to win me over with affectionate words and flirting. In fact, I was more annoyed with him because he was almost TELLING me when to rest and eat. How dare he? I rest and eat when I want to, not when a stranger tells me to. He was so annoying, patronising and pathetic. But I just loved listening to all his excuses and meaningless words. It was entertainment value to me on a cold wintry day in Yorkshire, after my boring day at work. This was better than any soap opera on television. I laughed to myself thinking of the old television programme called *On the Buses;* this was a version of *On the Oil Rigs*. It was a daily drama, and I loved it – just a bit too much.

CHAPTER 4

OPPORTUNITIES (LET'S MAKE LOTS OF MONEY)

I received the crescendo; the climax; the pinnacle; the sting. Just like I knew I would. The finale that Loy had been building up to all along for the past few months. He rang one night, pretending to be in tears. 'B-a-b-e, p-l-e-a-s-e, help me. I cannot get onto my internet banking. It tells me that I am abroad and will not let me access my bank account.' Then he added as a matter of fact to reiterate the situation: 'THAT'S because I am on the oil rigs.'

I pretended to be shocked. 'Surely not?' I exclaimed. I seriously deserved a blooming Oscar nomination for my unsympathetic responses and amateur acting ability. 'So what do other people on the oil rigs do? How do they access their online banking?'

He replied, stuttering, 'Er ... I-I-I am not sure. Sometimes, the banks are really funny about us accessing money overseas.'

I replied, 'But you are NOT overseas – you are only near Aberdeen, aren't you?'

'Yes ... yes, I am near Glasgow,' he said.

I replied, trying to hide another snigger, 'But, b-a-b-e, Glasgow is inland and has no oil rig. Did you mean ABERDEEN?'

'Yes, yes, sorry, it has been a long shift with flying the helicopter to the mainland and back. Yes, of course I meant Aberdeen,' he responded.

This was getting silly and I was now totally bored with him. 'Well, if you flew to the mainland, then why didn't you go to a bank in Aberdeen or wherever, to sort it out there then?' He didn't respond, as he probably couldn't find a quick enough answer or excuse.

I could tell he was getting impatient. Well, so was I. I left a long, deliberate, embarrassing pause for him to think of a reply. He suddenly burst out, almost shouting down the phone, 'LOOK, I AM on an oil rig and now need money for mechanical equipment.'

I replied, 'Oh, I thought you were there to do some helicopter and safety training?'

'Yes, yes, I am, but now they want me to help with a big project and it is worth millions of dollars, babe. It's a big opportunity then we can both share the money when the project is finished and we can live like kings and queens,' he wittered on, annoying me even more.

I responded, 'Ooh, that sounds really good, but in Aberdeen they use pounds and pence, not dollars.' He ignored this sarcastic and truthful comment.

'Yes, yes, it is good about the project ... but I desperately need to buy some equipment and, as you know, I cannot get to my bank account offshore, and if I do not buy this for the oil rig then I will ... WE WILL ... lose out on all this big money. Let me send you a link to the engineering company website, and the equipment I need for the rigs.'

'Oh, okay then,' I mumbled, secretly laughing at the stupidity and absurdity of it all. He forwarded a web address to me of an American industrial machinery site, along with a list of equipment to purchase. There were 10 x 3,000 litre steel fuel tanks and 15 x hydraulic crushers along with other items of heavy duty machinery. Total cost was over £250,000 converted from US dollars. I sent a message back, lying: *I am having issues with my internet at home, and the link. I thought you were on the rigs? How come you need all this heavy machinery? How is it going to get to the rigs? It is too heavy for a helicopter, and you only have a small helipad on the oil rig. Is it travelling to the rig by cargo ship? Do you pay additional shipping charges and import tax?*

All my inquisitive questions seemed to annoy him even more. He called me back straight away. I could tell he was trying to restrain himself from getting angry; his voice was getting louder and more animated. He almost shouted back, 'Look, I just NEED this important equipment sending to an address and I will forward it to you. It is Glasgow, you know, as I mentioned I work on the rigs in Glasgow, oh, and in Aberdeen.'

I chuckled to myself. Ooh yes, I had forgotten – Glasgow was now Aberdeen, but the oil rig number was based in Saudi Arabia ... his lies went on and on. He was full of bullshit, but he thought I believed him. I couldn't stop now; this had gone even further. The roles had changed in his cat and mouse game. I was now the cat, and HE was the desperate little mouse.

His loving text messages kept coming. He even rang to tell me that he loved me. I cringed at his words. He wanted me to say it to him, begging me like a small child. I refused point-blank, and he acted like he was pathetically crying. I loved my dead husband and no one would take his place for my love, and certainly not an idiot like scammer Loy, or whatever his name was. Loy wasn't quite as good an actor as I was, and certainly not as clever. I refused again to repeat his words, and I could tell he was now clutching at straws. 'Aww, babe, don't you love me – even a teeny, little bit?' he nagged.

'NO,' I replied loudly and rudely. 'I haven't even met you, and how DARE you put me in such a situation to try to cajole me into saying what YOU want to hear.' I cut the conversation off. He had now crossed the line, MY line, and it had to stop. He had now seriously pissed me right off. In fact, I was fucking fuming!

However, nothing stopped him, and he continued. Texting me again to reassure me that when the project that he had been specially selected to project manage was completed, he would be worth a lot of money, possibly millions. Then we could live together anywhere I wanted, in England. He even suggested that I should go house hunting immediately and look for a house up to £900,000 so we could all live together, happily ever after. But the caveat was that I had to consider selling MY house. I asked where he lived now. He stated, 'Luton.' Oh, a bit convenient as there is an airport there. Probably the only place he knew in England, along with Heathrow Airport. I said he would be better living nearer Heathrow if he was a long-haul pilot as the commute on the M25 would be horrendous, but of course, he would already know that. He responded that he was confused by my message. *Very convenient,* I thought. Yeah, he was now totally confused; confused about where he was, where he worked and even who he was. By the time I'd finished with him, he would be more than confused, he'd be bloody unhinged.

He still persisted with his messages, messaging me numerous times with pathetic comments. They were all ignored. Then suddenly he sent a message with an address for his expensive industrial machinery and equipment to be shipped to after I had ordered it online – this included his full name and address in PORT GLASGOW with a zip code, not a postcode! I was an expert on postcodes as you may recall from my first book in my youth. I googled it – the address was based in Kentucky, America. Hence him telling me he was in Glasgow; he meant *Port Glasgow* – he had even forgotten where the oil rig was! I drilled down further into Google Maps to see where the address was. I was laughing so much to myself. I now had the scammer's name (which was probably false), mobile phone number and even an address. I secretly congratulated myself. I did not reply to any further messages. I had had my fun and caught him out big time. Yes, the cat had caught the mouse; my job was done.

Unfortunately, the cat and mouse chase was still on for Loy, and he persisted. He was now like a dog with a bloody bone, never letting it drop. After all, he was expecting over £250,000 worth of heavy machinery to be paid for and delivered to Kentucky, a £900,000 house in Luton or somewhere in England, my hand in marriage and his alleged daughter to come and live with us – and we would all just live happily ever after. What an absolute loser. I cut off all contact but still viewed his messages, just out of curiosity.

The next day, dozens of messages came through from him, one after the other, repeatedly saying the same thing: *Don't let money come* between us both, but I do need money for this massive project, we will live a wealthy lifestyle when this project comes to an end ... We will want for nothing ... Why did you choose to break my heart? ... I love you so much ... We have such a strong connection ... Never leave me ... I am dying without you. Well at least if he died, then I would have peace and quiet – I like to think positively.

His drama and text messages went on and on. He even included emoji symbols of crying and sad faces. He rang me numerous times; I ignored every message and phone call. Eventually, after four weeks of him messaging me, telling me that I was heartless and had lost him his job, he gave up. Let some other woman have him and his declarations of true love and wanting to marry them. I was done with the game and now bored. The winner takes it all ... and it certainly wasn't him in this case.

Au revoir, Loy, and your airline pilot career – or was it oil rig worker, or helicopter pilot, project manager? Even he would forget his own lies when he called me. He was a blooming nutcase, trying to grind me down into giving him money, giving me his sob stories. It would never happen as I didn't have any money myself, never mind any to give away. I even thought about sending him a bill at his delivery address, for the hours spent on the phone with him and wasting MY time.

I now needed to focus on myself and other issues. I reported him to Tinder as a scammer, but as the main conversations about money had happened away from Tinder, on Hangouts, there was no real evidence, only my screenshots from Tinder of his profile picture and his Lufthansa aeroplane. Absolutely hilarious. He had already taken his profile down from Tinder after our initial conversation, as he had said he wanted to be 'faithful' to me! I sent his profile photo and write-up to Tinder anyway. I wasn't sure of the outcome, but my job was done. Now back to reality and real life.

Loy, your landing gear would never be going anywhere near my landing strip. You were just a flight of fancy – in your own head.

CHAPTER 5

ON THE FLOOR

I logged onto the dating apps, bored. James was single and available on Tinder. His profile picture looked gorgeous, and he looked, to me, a bit similar to Peter Andre, you know – that dark-haired and sexy, rugged look. He was maybe not quite as muscly as Peter, but he would do. James was quite a bit younger than me and looked very fit. He also didn't live too far away, in the West Yorkshire area. This was already looking very promising.

We messaged each other and he came over to see me. Parking his large white BMW in my driveway early one Sunday morning. We had a frothy coffee and a chat in my kitchen, and he casually dropped into the conversation that he had split up from his girlfriend and had two young children so had to be back home soon to collect them, as Sunday was his day for taking the children out.

Blooming heck, talk about being in a rush! I dismissed his initial conversation. He was either here to do the business, or he could just go back home. It was very early in the morning, flipping 7.30am. I was still tired; this was a SUNDAY morning, for goodness' sake. A girl needs some rest and I certainly needed my beauty sleep at my age. It had taken me over an hour to get ready and slap some make-up on to make myself look presentable and try to look younger than I actually was. And now here he was, giving me some talk about getting back home to take his kids out. I wished I hadn't bothered taking pride in my appearance. I seriously despaired of him but also respected him. At least he was honest and knew his responsibilities to his children. I had to give him some credit, I suppose.

We went upstairs; after all, I hadn't invited him over for just a frothy coffee and a chat. He had promised to buy me a McDonald's breakfast but had somehow 'forgotten' to stop at the local McDonald's just off the M62 motorway to collect one. He was in my bad books already. I wouldn't forgive him in the bedroom for being so lapse.

After an hour, he left to go back home. I was smirking to myself, a stupid childish smirk. That session was a bloody good way to start the day for a Sunday. He actually looked more tired when he left than I did. I tutted to myself as he drove away, his car leaving behind a massive oil stain on my newly laid drive. I would have to clean that up then. Here's to continuing with my housework and then having a restful day. Oh, and I had better change the bed sheets. I was feeling a bit tired myself and had to stop myself going for a little snooze.

I was relaxing at home later that evening when James messaged me, asking to come back to my house. His children had gone back to their mother after their visit, and he wanted a repeat of the morning session. *Hell, yeah, babe, just drive over here,* I texted back. I certainly wasn't going to drive all the way to the other side of Yorkshire to meet him. If he wanted it, then he came to mine; I told him I was a busy woman and jokingly said that he was lucky I had a 'spare slot' tonight – just for him. I rushed upstairs to slap more make-up on and look a bit more presentable. The sweatshirt and tight black leggings I was currently wearing would certainly put him off, not exactly a sexy feminine look. I changed into a nice dress to show off my cleavage.

Over the coming weeks, this became a regular Sunday morning arrangement, even if I had to get up early to slap, or rather 'cake', on make-up. It was hard work sometimes, as I looked like death warmed up when I woke up most mornings. It was a casual arrangement and that suited us both. After all, we were both single; we could do what the hell we wanted. It was our 'fix' to make us both feel good and get us through the day, before starting work on a mundane Monday morning. I even forgave him for his car leaking oil and lack of McDonald's breakfasts. He was too gorgeous to be angry with.

Suddenly, after a few months, the relationship went a bit awry. James was pushing my boundaries, and all my wrong buttons, in more ways than one. I was at home after work, and he suddenly sent me a photo of a pair of black lacy panties, randomly thrown on a bedroom floor. I messaged him back, puzzled, and asked whose they were. Apparently, they were his ex-girlfriend's as he had gone there to let the dog out. I wasn't sure if that was a double entendre. I wasn't even sure, and didn't even care, if they were her actual black lacy panties, or if he had just downloaded a photo off the internet. Whichever it was, it was bloody weird. I dismissed it, as I wasn't that bothered. After all, if I wanted a photo of some panties, I could just throw some of my own on the bedroom floor and use my iPhone to take a photo. He was such an idiot, but an attractive idiot.

He messaged me and asked me to save a pair of my own worn lacy panties, unwashed. Thinking I would be shocked or uncomfortable. He obviously didn't know that I had previously done the chatlines, so nothing shocked me anymore. I handed him a pair of my lacy panties when he next came to see me, making sure I had worn them all day at work, and then in the gym for an hour. That would serve him right as they weren't exactly as sweet-smelling as he probably expected. I sniggered to myself as he took the pair of red Ann Summers lacy panties, held them to his face and sniffed them, deeply. Even I wouldn't have done THAT – and they were my own! I watched him with a poker face but wanted to laugh so much. He was really pushing his luck. He was such a nice idiot, though, it was hilarious. This was now becoming a tit-for-tat game.

It also seemed to slightly agitate him even more that I wasn't really bothered and did anything he wanted me to. The next weekend, he messaged me with another strange request. Asking if he could clean my house – NAKED. I actually relished this scenario and immediately said enthusiastically, *Yes, of course, babe!* I decided I would let him clean my kitchen floor, as I hated cleaning it. With its white floor tiles, it always looked a bit grubby, even though it wasn't.

He stipulated that I had to wear a short leather mini skirt and high heels and tell him what to do. Yes, that could certainly be arranged, James! I encouraged this free cleaning request by sending him a photo of me wearing a tight miniskirt and skimpy top. He took the bait, like

I knew he would. I then sent him a photo of a bucket of soapy water and a car cleaning sponge that I had eventually found in my shed.

He suddenly rang me, full of feeble excuses and confessed meekly, 'Er ... I have never cleaned a kitchen floor before.'

I almost bellowed at him, 'YOU are KIDDING me? It's about time you bloody well learnt how to clean a floor then, naked, on your hands and knees, and don't forget all the grouting in between the tiles. I will get you an old toothbrush to scrub it clean.' He sounded shocked, as if this wasn't going quite to plan and he had a different erotic image in his head. I don't know what he had expected. A fantasy? No, this was reality. I told him again that my floor needed cleaning. He said maybe next week. He started this silly fantasy, so he could go through with it. I didn't let him forget about it and told him I hadn't cleaned this week as I was waiting for him with the sponge and soapy water. I sent him daily text messages and photos of a soapy sponge, just to remind him. I knew that I was now pushing HIS wrong buttons – and it served him right.

The next week, he rang me, sounding a bit more in control, with an addition to his fantasy. He would now come and clean my floor naked, but I had to show him how to do it first. 'Okay, babe, that can be arranged,' I said. But then I had to shout at him, as he hadn't done it correctly, and throw him out of my house into the front garden, slamming my door shut and locking it. I would be wearing a mini skirt and not a lot else. I just thought *What the heck?* and even wondered if he was drunk or had taken some substance.

Being a practical person, I asked him, what about his clothes and car keys? How would he get home over 50 miles away – naked and without his car? He hadn't quite thought about that. DID I let him in the house again? This wasn't a porn film, resulting in a young naked Peter Andre lookalike standing naked in a MILF's driveway, hiding behind the cars, with only a soapy car sponge and a bucket to cover his dignity. He was seriously unreal and deranged.

The other unfortunate thing about this scenario was that I lived on a busy main road, near a school and a bus stop. We would both possibly be reported for indecent exposure. He was now pushing MY bloody patience and my wrong buttons yet again. This wasn't happening. I was now tired of his fantasies, and I also needed a lie-in on Sunday mornings. After all, at my age, I needed all the beauty sleep I could get.

I never got my kitchen floor cleaned; I had to do it by myself, dressed. But I'm no scrubber, so I just might have to remind James to do it for me when he contacts me again..

CHAPTER 6

COLD AS ICE

I met up with William from Tinder. He came from South Yorkshire and wasn't even that good-looking, but on his profile write-up he mentioned that he had been to swingers' clubs. That would do – it was one of the items now on my crazy bucket list – to visit a swingers' club. He also put that he had plenty of timewasters on Tinder and to prove him wrong. People should know better than to dare me. So I sent him a random message, inviting him over.

By the following Sunday afternoon, he was at my house, upstairs in my spare bedroom in bed. We didn't kiss or even really talk that much; we both really knew this was an 'arrangement' to suit us both. I wasn't that bothered about kissing him. He had set the rules so I respected that, as goodness knows who he had been with before me. Gone was the comfort of kissing just one man. I had to accept everyone was different and that he did not want to kiss me before having sex, however strange and emotionally cold it seemed.

We arranged to go to a swingers' club in Leeds the next weekend. It was cheaper to join as a couple, so we decided that we would join as a joint membership and do our own thing inside the club but still look out for each other, make sure that we were both safe. The arrangement was that he would always walk me to my car in the club car park afterwards; just to be sure I was okay.

I was intrigued about a swingers' club and obviously would never have joined one with my husband – we weren't into sharing or even looking at any other person. There was no need to as we were in love. We weren't all about sex, or, in our case, making love. We had much more of a connection than that. But now, here I was, waiting in my car, in the swingers' club car park, too scared to go inside. I hadn't been into any club for many years, the last one possibly being in the late 1980s before I married the first time. It certainly wasn't this type of club; it was a normal nightclub in Hull city centre.

William eventually met me in the car park, and we entered the club, registered our names and paid as new members. We both walked down the darkened corridor and opened the heavy door to the club. I wasn't sure what I expected to see. Naked bodies, writhing around, having sex in front of me? Well, no, it wasn't like the image I had in my head at all. Inside the club it was just like a normal pub with a pool table and bar. The club management showed us around and into the available playrooms, a bondage room and a room with a two-way mirror where people could observe, along with a massive playroom – which I took to really mean 'a massive bloody free-for-all'. There was a large hot tub that William pulled a face at; he said he dreaded to think what was in the water! There was a large sign stating that no sex was allowed in the hot tub, but some people were definitely heavy petting, shall we say. I wasn't used to seeing naked people in a hot tub. The only hot tub I had been to previously was at the local gym, and I am certain that Total Fitness and David Lloyd fitness centres didn't have naked people in them! No way would I be going into that pool with everything private showing! It was a bit daunting, I must admit; I had never seen groups of people naked before.

I wasn't into porn and hadn't seen any since I was twenty years old and with my then boyfriend, Jeff. We were young and watched soft porn just to get us in the mood for sex at his house. I remembered they were actually his dad's VHS videos that he borrowed from mates at work at Blue Circle Cement. We just watched it for fun, you know – the 1970s stuff with hairy fannies and ridiculous storylines, usually involving teachers and female students, or some tradesman and a frustrated housewife, as I remember. But here in the swingers' club, porn was showing on each TV in every room, and not a hairy fanny in sight. There was no sound, but I got the idea. Not hardcore porn, just soft porn with a bit of anal literally shoved in for good measure. Films of women pretending to enjoy themselves – well, they would, wouldn't they, as they got paid for it. Take it from me, if I got paid mega money to have weird sex with strangers and be filmed, I would have a bloody big smile on my face. I had to guess what noises were being made as the televisions were on mute – but yeah ... I could guess.

We both just had to have sex in one of the club's private rooms. We might as well get our money's worth, we thought. I made sure we chose a room with a lock on the inside, as I could hear people walking around and talking outside the room, then trying the door handle to see if it was unlocked. Jeez, talk about being a bit off-putting. The club became addictive in many ways.

However, the swingers' club was 'safe sex'. Safe in that there were security staff there, and safe that everyone had to register to become a member. It was safer than using dating apps and having random men at my house. I realised I had been lucky so far. I hadn't been attacked, raped or murdered. The club environment was safer. The sex was optional. I learnt not to judge the people that went there. How could I judge them – when I was bloody well there myself!

Welcome to the world of swinging ...

CHAPTER 7
ONE STEP BEYOND

Foolishly, I couldn't resist, and I put myself back out there, in the public domain, and now on Instagram, just to 'dip my toe in the water', so to speak. I had never used Instagram before. I didn't want to show a photo of my face on my profile picture so just put a photo of my feet in some very nice red high-heeled shoes.

Ironically, I had always hated my feet as they had high arches and were far too big for my height. Suddenly now on Instagram, men seemed to like my big, clumsy, freaky size 7 to 8 feet, and I had now received hundreds of 'likes' on my account, and numerous messages. Some men were so crude with their messages and wanted me to put my toes and feet in places I would never even have dreamt of. Some of the suggestions were a physical impossibility. But I had been on the chatlines so was used to that kind of talk. Nothing really surprised me anymore.

Jake was from the Leeds area and contacted me through Instagram. He said he loved foot worship, had done it loads of times, and was looking to carry on with his feet fetish. He revealed the extent of his fetish by telling me that his ex-girlfriend had dominated him and made him sleep at her feet at nighttime. He said he hardly got any sleep but enjoyed it. He loved everything about feet, especially hard skin on heels. In my mind, I knew this conversation was now getting slightly out of control, but I had to carry on. I was totally absorbed and mesmerised by his revelations and actions.

We took the conversation away from Instagram. He confessed over his messages that his ex would use a foot file to smooth away the hard skin on her feet and would save the shavings and even her toenail clippings. Then when she plated up his tea, she would sprinkle the dry, dusty, powdery feet shavings and clippings on top of his food and watch him eat it. He said it didn't bother him; he enjoyed it and asked her to do it even more. This apparently even continued if they went to a restaurant, where she would take a container of her nail clippings and sprinkle it over his food. I couldn't believe it. In public? In a restaurant? Surely not? Even in private it seemed bad enough, but he was deadly serious. I looked online at the feet fetish market and it opened my eyes, and feet, to a totally different world. As usual, my inquisitive mind was working overtime. I was intrigued and just had to know more.

He messaged me again, wanting to worship my feet. I knew this was another level completely and way out of my depth. But I felt compelled to say yes, just out of fascination and curiosity. He now had specific demands. I read his message with a mixture of intrigue but also horror. He wanted to suck my toes through my tights, and then take my tights off and suck each toe. Licking between each toe, before moving on to nibbling the hard skin on my heels and licking my high arches. I suddenly felt a bit guilty as I had no experience of foot worship and felt I had led him on. Did it lead to sex? I hadn't a clue. All I could do was reply in a message, *Okay, babe, but can I keep my panties on?* He replied, Yes. Things had now gone too far for me to back out graciously; after all, he thought I had done this before. At least the boundaries were set and I could keep my panties on. As if that was any consolation in this bizarre situation! There was no way I could get out of this without upsetting or offending him. I was going to have to go through with it.

I asked him to send me a photo of himself, which he did, and I was quite impressed. He was younger than me, slim and attractive, with a sexy, cheeky grin. He was actually quite cute. I grinned to myself. This was going to be a Sunday afternoon never to be forgotten in my house. I wasn't sure if it was for the wrong or right reasons but now didn't care as this was definitely bloody going ahead, come hell or high water.

Jake arranged to come round to my house. He had asked me to dress up as if I was at work in the office; he liked the 'secretary look'. My office attire did not usually consist of black sheer tights, a black leather mini skirt, a tight black blouse with my cleavage hanging out and red high heels with peep toes showing my bright red nail varnish on my toenails – but it blooming well did that day! Let him believe that was how I looked when I went to my workplace in the office. I knew for a fact that if I wore that outfit to work, my managing director would have words with me and then send me home to change into attire more 'appropriate and suitable for the office'. I wouldn't blame him either. I sniggered to myself at even the thought of walking across the company car park the way I was dressed now.

When I opened my front door to Jake, he looked me up and down and gave me a cheeky, sexy grin, just like on his photograph. I suppose I did look a bit classy (for once) as I had my long wavy hair highlighted in a rich golden colour and wore lots of make-up to hide my wrinkles, which were slightly visible again, in between my Botox appointments. He said that he liked my 'secretary look' and loved my red high heels. Unfortunately, I had to take my shoes off to go up my stairs to the bedroom; otherwise, I would have fallen over and possibly broken an ankle or both legs. I also didn't want to damage my new wooden flooring in the hallway with delves from heel marks. I was still a practical woman at heart. A girl has to think of these things.

I really didn't know what to expect. Luckily, he led the conversation as we both went into the spare bedroom. Him telling me, slowly, that he would like to start off by touching and stroking my feet. Okay, that was fine. I had put my shoes back on in the bedroom for the effect he wanted. I sat on the side of the bed and he was on his knees, in front of me, taking off my shoes and sniffing them, inhaling slowly and deeply. I had to stifle a giggle. After all, I didn't want to offend him, and he definitely looked even more bloody cute and sexy close up.

Jake suddenly asked a question that I wasn't expecting. Could HE take off his clothes? Jeez. That wasn't in the rules, or in his messages. I had been so concerned about staying dressed myself that I didn't even think about him being naked. Shit. I now had to think quickly. I cleared my throat and said in a pathetic girly whisper, 'Yes, of course you can, babe,' just like it was a natural answer. As if I was used to having my feet worshipped by a naked sexy man, who I now really wanted to have sex with.

He stripped off in front of me. I couldn't help looking at his toned body, and obviously the most interesting hard part of his body. Here he was, bloody sex on legs, like a Chippendale dancer, right in front of me, literally at my feet. I felt myself getting turned on and restrained myself by biting my lip so much that it flipping hurt. He was still on his hands and knees, his clothes abandoned, tossed onto the bedroom floor in a heap. This was now becoming like a porn scene.

He continued to slowly caress my feet, every inch of them; toes, heels, instep. It felt quite soothing, calming and warm, but I wasn't here to relax. I had to be in some control; anything could happen. He then began stroking my ankles and telling me how slim and nice they were. I took off my tights as he requested, and he began sucking each toe, quite hard so it wasn't ticklish. Then slowly began licking the area between each toe. It was an unusual sensation but felt quite nice and warm.

He asked me to call him 'Foot Slave' or 'Slave', and to say this aggressively after each sentence. Goodness knows what my neighbours would think if they could hear all this through the bedroom walls. Foot Slave was now nibbling at the hard skin on my heels. He reminded me of a little rabbit or guinea pig, eating a carrot, gnawing and nibbling away contentedly. I tried to put that image out of my mind as he had now stopped nibbling and had started licking my feet. This was much better than any paid-for foot massage or reflexology session. My feet felt lovely and smooth, almost like having a soothing pedicure.

I could see he was getting more and more sexually excited as the time went on; he had been licking, nibbling and sucking my feet for over half an hour. Then he asked if he could cum. Bloody hell, I didn't expect THAT question either. In fact, I didn't really know what questions to expect. I was still partially dressed. After all – rules are rules. Even though my panties were on, my tights were off and my blouse was now fully undone to reveal my black lacy bra and large cleavage. I was getting bloody hot in that bedroom, in more ways than one! I needed to open a window to let some cool air into the room to cool me down, but I daren't move and spoil his moment.

Foot Slave was still knelt on the floor, naked. With my right foot deep in his mouth, he quickly ejaculated into his cupped hand. I watched in amazement, not sure what to say or even do. Afterwards, he went to the bathroom, got washed, dressed, kissed me urgently on my mouth, thanked me and left. The joke 'eats, shoots and leaves' suddenly sprung into my mind.

I watched him drive away as I stood at my front doorway, almost stunned. Did that genuinely just happen? It must have done as my feet felt like I was walking on air. They were now clean and smooth with no hard skin.

We have kept in touch by messages, but I haven't seen Foot Slave since that day. If you are reading this, Foot Slave, my feet could do with another personal pedicure and licking clean, please ... After all, these feet were made for walking, not wanking over.

CHAPTER 8

SULTANS OF SWING

I met Marc at a local swingers' club. I didn't originally see his face; the first body part that I saw was his large black cock that was half erect and poking through a glory hole in the club. The words 'soft, strong and very long', just like the toilet paper advert, certainly sprung into my mind. I walked further into the darkened glory hole room and closed the heavy black door behind me. The guy I was with that afternoon, my fuck buddy, also went behind the glory hole wall; his was the size of a tiddler compared to this large one. I went down onto my knees, and you can probably guess the rest.

When I finished, I left the room quickly. After all, the bloke with the big cock didn't have a clue who was on the other side of the glory hole, as that was the idea. I was almost skipping down the corridor of the club, with my white towel still around me, laughing to myself. I was just so bad and it was so funny; well, it was to me anyway. I was such a tease but didn't care. They loved it; after all, that's why they were there. To be teased and pleased.

This was a great way to spend my Sunday afternoon and early evening in my opinion, especially after all my mental anguish and legal crap I had to endure over the last few months. It also took my mind off the thought of going to work the next day. Every working day there was now a helpdesk day, manning the phones and talking all day and correcting software problems. As much as I loved helping people and had genuinely met some lovely people, it absolutely bored the shit out of me and was now making me depressed. But I knew it was a stable job and provided an income to pay my mortgage, bills and everyone else's debts that I had accumulated over the last year. *Just add it onto Helen's blooming accruing debts,* I thought. I was so much in debt that I knew there was no way out, so didn't worry anymore. I now had acceptance of my tragic situation.

Today, I was in my self-destruct mode, which was bloody dangerous, to others and myself. But I had to carry on regardless, thinking out loud that it was like the song *Sex & Drugs & Rock & Roll*. I certainly didn't do drugs, so I just chose the 'Sex & Rock & Roll'. Hence, I was in the swingers' club. Now looking at an uncertain future, and the even more unpredictable lifestyle of a brazen slapper, that I readily admitted – which was even more worrying.

I knew that after the euphoria, wild, extreme behaviour, being in control and dominating, unfortunately came the consequences. The crashing down of emotions, usually the next day. The despondency, hopelessness and grief. The reality that I had no one to talk to, no one to hold me tight when I cried and tell me that everything would be all right. As the reality was that it would NEVER be all right ever again, however much I cried. Andrew was gone, and that hurt more than anyone could know. I knew I had lost him and was now losing my fucking mind, and I just couldn't help myself or my actions anymore.

I had had a busy day already that Sunday. Mechanic Boy had come round earlier to my house when he should really have been food shopping for his wife and kids. We only had time for a quickie on the black leather sofa in my living room. I couldn't be bothered to wash the bedding anyway on my nice clean spare bed upstairs, so the sofa suited me just fine. We were supposed to be over with, finished, but he just couldn't keep away.

When he had left, I had a quick shower, washed my hair again then drove into Leeds to meet my so-called fuck buddy, William, at the swingers' club. At the bar, we each had a soft drink then went into a private locked room for a quickie; after all, we had both paid to get into the club, so we might as well get some enjoyment from it and some value for our money.

After our quickie, we both went back to the bar area, and I saw a bloke who had caught my eye earlier. He was cheeky and knew it; he was definitely the rude, crude type. The 'love 'em and leave 'em' kind of guy, I could easily tell. That was okay, as I was now the female version of him. He was sitting alone, already drunk and drinking spirits, watching porn on the TV screens. He had a lingering odour of smoke around him, so obviously a smoker. I usually hated the smell of smoke lingering on clothes, skin and hair, but suddenly it seemed quite attractive to me, along with the heady alcohol smell. I was seriously losing all my morals and common sense.

We both began talking to the drunk smoker, just making polite conversation. I didn't even ask his name. To be honest, I didn't even care what his name was; I just wanted his slim tattooed body. He was looking me up and down even though I had my white towel still wrapped around me. Underneath, I was wearing a black front lace-up basque, stockings and black panties. I never showed everything off; I didn't feel the need to. All three of us talked, but he was only interested in me. He flirted, grinned and gave me a quick wink. I guessed this was a sign he wanted things to go further. We both snuck off to a playroom and I left my fuck buddy sat alone in the bar area. He would hopefully hook up with a female or two and enjoy himself.

In the playroom, I took off my towel and laid it on the plastic sheeted bed, ready for the inevitable. We were both going to use and abuse each other, and I didn't even bloody care. I had already had Mechanic Boy and my fuck buddy earlier, and given someone a blow job in the glory hole. I was sure I could entertain more. I was now singing *Let Me Entertain You*, the Robbie Williams song, in my head. So here he was, MY entertainment. A drunk smoker boy – this was a bloody good day. Unfortunately, I had forgotten that the playroom Smoker Boy had chosen for us had a two-way mirror.

He was absolutely pissed and being rough, which I hated. He began hair pulling, spitting at me and trying to pin me down with his hands and legs. Then he grabbed me by my throat. I was fucking fuming. I could be as rough with him then and would certainly give him something to remember me by. I began stabbing my sharp fingernails into his back and buttocks and scratching downwards on his back, hard, like a frenzied cat on a scratching post. I was sure I must have drawn blood as his skin was under my fingernails. He was far too drunk to even notice or even cum, so goodness knows why he had even gone to the swingers' club. We took it in turns to hurt and humiliate each other. I had to seriously stop myself from slapping or hitting him, hard, to get rid of all my pent-up anger over the past year. I knew if I had slapped him that I possibly wouldn't be able to stop myself, and I wasn't even a violent person. I had to get a grip and restrain myself; otherwise, this could turn into a full-scale fight, and it certainly wouldn't all be Smoker Boy's fault.

The shagging, spitting, humiliation and BDSM had gone on long enough, I decided. I slid my legs away from him and moved off the bed. Sometimes, you just have to admit defeat; we had had our fun – if you could call it fun! Heaven knows what that display was. He was drunk, I was turning aggressive, and it could have easily got out of hand. Luckily, in the club there were bouncers and security to intervene if things went too far. I didn't want it to go that far.

We amicably parted company – him yanking off his condom, almost in disgust, throwing it in the bin in the corner and walking out of the room, leaving me to clean the plastic beds with spray disinfectant, wet wipes and industrial blue roll. But that's the reality of a swingers' club, easy come – easy go, in more ways than one! I smirked as I looked at the massive red scratch marks on his back as he walked away, not even saying goodbye.

Just then, the door opened and a man walked in. 'Shall I help you clear up?' he asked.

'No, it's okay, don't worry,' I replied, not even looking up, spraying the bed thoroughly with disinfectant and drying it hurriedly with the blue roll, ready for the next people.

'It wasn't very nice of that guy to just leave you to clear up, but that was quite an impressive performance,' he said, nodding in the direction of the mirror. Shit, I had forgotten about the two-way mirror as I had never used that room before. Goodness knows who had been watching that display of a violent BDSM porn show. If I had known that, I would have acted more like a porn star and put even more effort into it. I was now sweating from wearing my ridiculously tight basque, and my usually nicely groomed hair was now a mess, as if I had just got out of bed in the morning. I daren't even think about my make-up, which was probably smeared across my face.

He suggested going into a more private room, without the two-way mirror, and with a door that locked. I found my panties, which had been abandoned on the floor, and put my towel around me again, which was now damp, and followed him, barefoot, trotting like a pony on tiptoes, into another room down the corridor. He bolted the door and dropped his white towel onto the floor, and I could then tell he was the man behind the glory hole wall, who I had given a blow job to earlier. He introduced himself as Marc. Unfortunately for me, he was just too big in a certain area. It was literally like putting a square peg into a round hole! It just wouldn't, and physically couldn't, fit in properly, however many times we tried over the next half hour. Now seemed like an ideal time to get dressed and go home. I had the stress of work the next day. Oh, and Fuck Buddy didn't manage to pull anyone. He was still sat near the bar, all alone watching the porn, whilst all my X-rated performances were happening in the rooms behind him.

I went into the changing rooms and quickly got dressed, paid for the drinks and walked to my car in the club car park, alone. I had seriously given up with Fuck Buddy. He was in a mood and had left already. He had broken our arrangement and I was not happy. Suddenly my mobile phone started ringing. Mobiles weren't allowed in the club; mine had been in the club locker for a couple of hours. I noticed I had numerous missed phone calls. Shit. One was from Danny, the young fit Turkish man from a posh area of Leeds. He was bloody gorgeous, as well as rich – and he was ringing now.

'H-e-e-e-e-y, babe,' he said when I answered my phone. My heart just melted when he rang me; he was so sexy, it was unbelievable. 'Are you home?' Shit. I had to think quickly.

'No, babe, I am just leaving a friend's house but will be home in about an hour. Are you coming over to see me?' I answered.

'Hell, yeah, babe, I have missed you.'

'Same here,' I replied. 'Let me just drive home and have a quick shower then I will be ready for you. Shall I wear those black stockings you like, and my new black lacy bra?'

'Hell, yeah, babe. I can't wait. See you soon,' he replied. I could tell he was chewing some gum as he was talking. That made him even sexier to me and I couldn't wait to see him and his naked slim, sexy body. He was a man of few words. What did that matter when he had such a gorgeous body and was such a soft kisser? He always turned me on.

Okay, I had better stop daydreaming and get a move on and drive home quickly on that motorway, get showered and change yet again, ready for the next session. After all, the government does recommend '5 portions a day'. I would be having my 5 portions today, but it certainly wouldn't be of fruit and vegetables.

CHAPTER 9

FADE TO GREY

It was April 2022 when I received the phone call from Castle Hill Hospital that my mother was seriously ill and had been admitted to their hospital for care. The sister or nurse rang me from the ward. She obviously did not know the situation, or history, between my mother and myself. I told her that I would come to the hospital and speak to her. I didn't want to be telling her about family arguments and disputes; these were busy professional people.

I drove with some trepidation to the hospital, did the usual COVID ritual of sanitising my hands and wearing a mask and went into the lift, up to the relevant ward. The sister on the ward took me aside into a private room to talk, told me that my mother was ill and explained some medical diagnosis. I was only half listening. Apparently, her gall bladder and stomach issues were now incurable; the other words she said meant she had cancer and not long to live. I didn't even know she had anything wrong with her gall bladder or stomach, and I don't think my mother did either.

I admit that some of her words just washed over me, as all I was thinking was *do I see her or not?* Suddenly the sister asked me the same question. She was asking me in a whisper, so I knew it was serious. After all, I was in the room that had a tissue box in it. That bloody 'tissue box of death'. Just like when my father died in hospital all those years ago, and Mother and I were ushered into a quiet room – with a tissue box, one tissue poking out of the top for easy access for when you are sobbing uncontrollably. I knew from that moment that my mother's death was imminent. But I wasn't sobbing. I had a slight tear in my right eye but managed to move my blue COVID face mask upwards slightly to catch it. It acted like blotting paper and was useful for hiding tears. I had found that out over the past year, especially at Andrew's funeral.

'Did you wish to see your mother?' she quietly asked me again.

For some unexplained reason, I didn't even hesitate and replied, 'Yes, I have to have closure.' She nodded sympathetically and said that I had got there just in time. I wasn't sure what she meant by time. Did she mean minutes, hours, days, weeks, months? I was too scared to even ask.

She called a nurse over to assist, and the nurse took me to the individual room where Mother was laid flat on her back, looking upwards to the ceiling; she could not sit up or move her legs. Her hair was longer than I remembered, and she looked weak and frail and had lost weight. She hadn't been to the hairdresser's for years to have her usual poodle perm, making her look like the Queen or Queen Mother (when they were alive), but what did that matter now? It didn't. The nurse went over to my mother and said quietly, 'Your daughter is here to see you.' My mother turned to the side to look at me. The nurse kindly brought me a blue plastic visitor's chair and I sat next to her bed. I felt very uncomfortable, unnerved and still unwanted.

I didn't know what to say. She was always difficult to talk to, and I usually got very little reply, if any. I tried to act upbeat and the words just blurted out. 'Hi, how are you? Have you missed me?' After the family argument and her slamming the phone down on me numerous times and refusing to talk to me, I hadn't seen her for two years. But I wasn't going to mention that.

'Yes, where have you been?' she asked. I said I hadn't been very well with sickness. Which wasn't a lie; she had no idea that Andrew had died and then I had been diagnosed with a tumour and had had recent major surgery. It was nothing to do with her as it was my life, and my business, not hers.

She had made it quite clear all those years ago that she wanted nothing to do with me. The words *I despise you* are what she had said previously, along with what she had shouted at me when I was young, about twelve years old: *I hope you rot in hell.* Yes, those words were what she thought about her only daughter, me. No wonder I was mentally deranged and bloody unhinged. If I had told Mother last year that Andrew had died, I know she wouldn't have shown any sympathy. If anything, she would have gloated. I knew never to show any emotion or weakness as she relished it, almost thriving on it.

Andrew had originally given my mother the benefit of the doubt, saying that no one could be that bad. A couple of years into our relationship, he soon changed his mind and said I had been right all along, saying she was a mean, nasty, spiteful, evil witch – I agreed. That was the truth. I said to him, laughing at his disbelief, 'Andrew, you know me. I am always right, never wrong. I told you so. I even warned you!' After that, he called her 'The Witch'. To be honest, that was polite compared to what some people have called her.

There was a comb on her bedside cabinet. I slowly combed her hair. I'm not really sure why, but I just wanted to make her look a bit more presentable, or like the mother I used to remember. I asked if she wanted a drink as there were some high protein drinks in beakers next to her bed, and I helped her have a few sips of one. I wanted to cry but had to hold it back. She had her own bathroom in her hospital room. I said I just needed to use the toilet for a quick wee. There was a sign on the door stating the bathroom was for patients only. Stuff that. *Rules are there to be broken,* I thought to myself. In the bathroom, I admit I did cry, big bloody tears, as I knew she was at the end of her life.

I wondered how much more I could take with all the grief. One by one, everyone seemed to be dying. I wiped my tears as I looked at her possessions: a jacket and handbag both placed inside a hospital plastic bag, hung up on the coat pegs in her own little bathroom. I knew she wouldn't ever be wearing that jacket, or using her handbag, ever again. After a few minutes, I came out of the bathroom, with red blotchy eyes, and sat with her again. I left an hour later; I told her I would be back in a couple of days. I stuck to my word. The nurses kindly letting me stay as long as I liked, even after visiting time, as they knew I lived a distance away. I will be forever grateful for their genuine care and empathy. This routine was to continue for the next few weeks. It was tiring, but she was my mother. I didn't know how long she had to live; no one truly knew. I carried on visiting, trying to forget how she had previously treated me and how much she had hurt me with her vindictive words and her physical violence. I had nothing to prove but knew I was a more compassionate person than she had ever been in her life. I could still hold my head up high; she couldn't.

The whole sorry situation gave me mixed thoughts and emotions. I was absolutely shattered; all the sadness and grief of the past year was now taking its toll and I suddenly needed some breathing space. Mother made it even worse by telling the nurses that she did not want any of her family to know she was even in hospital. Her brother and sister still lived locally, but she was adamant they weren't to know anything about her illness. Even the nurses took me aside and quietly said that I really should tell the family. I said that she never really associated with them. In fact, she never associated with anyone, was unsociable and had no friends, and as much as she was a pain, I had to respect her wishes. I guessed from the nurses' concerns that she hadn't long to live; it was now a traumatic waiting game. The game of imminent death.

CHAPTER 10

ERASE/REWIND

It was now May 2022 and I had hit another massive low; it was exactly a year since Andrew died. The first year is always the worst for memories – or so people constantly reminded me. The first anniversary of their death, the first Christmas without them, their birthday, our wedding anniversary, Valentine's Day – the list was endless. Whichever date or occasion it was, I certainly knew I wouldn't be receiving a card ever again with a handwritten message inside ending *love you always, from Andrew XXXXX*

My friends obviously made a big fuss on my birthday, Christmas and special occasions, with beautiful cards and presents exchanged, along with nice meals in restaurants. I appreciated and loved my friends more than I had ever done before. But I still went home to an empty house. I had to get a grip and realise that my life had now changed. I didn't really want to go out most of the time but had to try and be sociable. When I did venture out, I suddenly wanted to be back at home, but when I was at home I didn't want to be there either and would wonder why I had rushed home. It was a strange, uncertain feeling, possibly a feeling of abandonment. The realisation that I WAS alone now, by myself – forever. I tried not to wallow in self-pity, but it was bloody hard some days.

Only my true friends had seen me at my mental breakdown stage; my constant sobbing, which sounded even worse and more harrowing the more my friends hugged me in sympathy. Although I was grateful, their sympathy and compassion made me despair even more. I just needed Andrew back. Good old dependable and reliable Andrew, the person who didn't like to see me cry, as he knew I didn't cry easily, and the one who would always support me in whatever I did. He had been my foundation and rock in my life, more than anyone would ever know. I needed stability, and he gave me that. I certainly wasn't mentally stable anymore.

I needed a bloody miracle and that would never happen. I was going out of my mind, sobbing uncontrollably each day, telling myself that I was so incompetent and useless as I couldn't even save my own husband. The whole turmoil of that fateful night playing out constantly, over and over in my mind. This continual repeat and rewind was driving me fucking insane, even a year later. It was like an old VHS video, playing constantly in my head. It was relentless and I daren't close my eyes to even sleep. I wanted to erase it, but I also didn't. I also wanted to remember as it was the last time I had seen Andrew alive. In my head were the continual flashbacks to the frantic shouting, the screaming, the swearing with frustration and, most of all, MY fucking incompetence.

I would live with this for the rest of my life. I had tried so hard to save him and asked myself over and over just how the hell I could let my husband die in front of me. Every day, I blamed myself. My PTSD I had as a child now coming to the forefront of my mind. I would now add this new trauma to the mix. I was going out of my bloody mind with trauma and grief, and I seriously knew it. I had to keep busy with any distraction, just so I didn't think about that horrific night.

I randomly looked at Facebook; there were 'grief kind' and 'grieving' groups. People had suffered like myself; I wasn't the only one and I knew that. I made a comment to someone, saying I felt the same way with grief. This one single comment then opened up a new world – to the scammers. I suddenly got friend requests from strangers living all over the world. Not surprisingly, they were all men, with the same comments or the same story: *I know how you feel as my wife recently died ... I still have her car as I cannot even think about selling it ... Does the pain ever go?* What the fucking hell! These men were fucking unreal. I deleted my comment along with their so-called 'Friend Requests'. I may as well go back to scammer Loy and his oil rig! It was the same level, trying to scam the vulnerable and grieving. Forget that shit.

I then went against all my principles and reached out for help. I rang for an appointment with a proper grief counsellor through work's private health insurance. I wish I hadn't bothered. I should have trusted my instincts; they were usually right. After I'd waited a week for a telephone appointment, a woman called me back. I tried not to cry as I briefly explained the three sudden bereavements, my operation and the fact that I still had to work but felt I couldn't cope most days. She replied that it was too soon to help me and if I had a pen and paper she would recommend a certain book for me to read about bereavement. For Fuck's Sake! Was SHE for fucking real? I wasn't a child, and I had waited a bloody week for this shambolic, unhelpful, ridiculous response. I lied when I said I was writing down the book title and author. I knew she could tell by my attitude that I wasn't impressed with her so-called 'grief counselling'.

The only constructive and accurate thing she quoted, and I agreed with, was 'work have unrealistic expectations of you in your circumstances'. She had hit the nail right on the bloody head! That quote was so true. Unfortunately, she then let herself down by advising me to contact the Samaritans if I was desperate. I sighed. I didn't need the Samaritans. I needed a quick fix, something that the Samaritans certainly couldn't give me.

I put the phone down and, in defiance, I logged straight onto the dating apps. That would show the stupid cow. I didn't need her non-existent grief counselling, to read a book, or to contact the Samaritans. I needed a bloody miracle, which was never going to happen, and most of all I needed sex to make me feel wanted, empowered and in control. Stuff her advice. As usual, I would make my own way in life and do whatever I wanted. That was the last time I would ever reach out to anyone. Yes, I should have trusted my instincts. I was annoyed with myself; in fact, I was fucking fuming with myself!

CHAPTER 11

DRIVER'S SEAT

I needed a quick fix, a distraction. Anything to take my mind off the anniversary of Andrew passing, my unstable life and everything! I had nothing left. I was now becoming an even harder, arrogant bitch to blot out the reality of my life. I was on a continual rollercoaster of debt, self-harm, addictions and compulsive sexual behaviour along with my anxiety, irritability and anger ... my list went on and on. I was a psychiatrist's, or psychologist's, ideal patient. But in my mind I knew I had to carry on regardless, as the truth was that no one could help me. That had been made very clear by the so-called 'grief counsellor', whose 'counselling' had made me more grief-stricken than before. My sick note for bereavement when Andrew died had been done over the phone via a doctor's receptionist, no questions asked, no follow-up or offer of any help. I now knew I hadn't much chance of seeing anyone who could help. I would learn by my own mistakes, just like I had when I was a young child.

I logged onto Tinder and found Ian. He looked okay, not my usual type, but okay. He was only slightly younger than me. Hopefully, he would be mature then. His profile said he was married and *'looking for fun'*.

The usual then, I thought. I sighed to myself and shrugged my shoulders. In other words, that meant *'my wife doesn't want sex anymore, so I need an affair'.* I liked the challenge; after all, I had the upper hand, if you excuse the pun. He had a blurry photo showing on Tinder but sent me a nice holiday photo of him in Miami – no doubt taken by his wife. He said he was a businessman and lived locally. I asked if he had done this kind of thing before. *God, yeah, babe ... loads,* he put on his reply message back, as if it was a common weekly practice, like popping to the supermarket for a weekly shop. These men have no shame. If I found out my husband was doing half the stuff these married men do on Tinder, I would go ballistic and throw him out. But hey – I had no husband anymore so could do whatever I liked, with who the hell I liked.

I gave him my address and we arranged to meet at my house. On that day, he messaged back saying he was parked outside but he daren't come up my driveway in his car. He was scared. For goodness' sake! This was the person who allegedly did this kind of thing – ALL THE TIME! I knew he was lying; he wasn't an expert at this at all. But I bloody well was. We met somewhere neutral so he wouldn't be 'so scared', in a local industrial estate car park that was so seedy, it was laughable. He was in his large Mercedes, me in my new Audi. Bought on finance in a flippant, compulsive and mental meltdown moment. I was past caring, so fuck it.

My car was the only thing I had actually bought for myself for over ten years. I told myself that I deserved it. Both private registration plates spelt our names, so we knew there was no lying on what we were called. I could usually get away with a false name by parking my car down the street when I had a 'visitor', but not this time. I parked up next to his car and climbed into his passenger seat. He was sat in the driver's seat and said he was nervous. Bloody hell – shouldn't that be the other way round? I should be the nervous one. I looked at him and said to him that he had instigated this 'meeting' and it was up to him. I was busy and didn't have time for games. We talked for a few minutes and I said to decide if he fancied me or not. If not, then we would forget this liaison ever happened and no hard feelings. I would just walk or, in this case, drive away.

I leant over to him and kissed him hard and passionately then put my hand on his groin. Yeah, something was definitely hard there, and it certainly wasn't his feelings. Just to give him a little taster of what he was missing. Call it a 'warm-up'. I then got out of his car and back into mine. It was now his decision. I took no prisoners. The answer was either a yes or no. Yeah, I was in the driver's seat before this relationship had even started, not him, and I knew it. He didn't know it – yet.

Not surprisingly, I received a message from him very early the next morning. These men were so fickle and easily led, it was laughable, but I liked to be in control. Apparently, he would be coming round to my house and hadn't been able to stop thinking about me all night. His requests were that he wanted me to wear only tights, tie him to a chair and do a lap dance in front of him. Well, at least the tights would hide the deep scars and stretch marks on my stomach, so an advantage to me there. As you can imagine, not all of this happened. Yes, I admit, I did wear sheer tights. I knew all he really wanted was to go to bed for a quick session – tights or no tights. No time even for a private lap dance or to tie him to a chair! My lap-dancing skills would be very limited anyway, possibly resembling a dancing baby elephant more than a graceful stripper. A quickie suited me; after all, I was a busy woman.

He was a precarious one, though, as he then confessed to having a heart condition. Jeez. My imagination was now running riot thinking all scenarios such as – what if he had a medical episode at my house or in the bedroom? What would I say when the paramedics arrive? I didn't know his full name, date of birth, or even where he lived. Then we would be caught out big time. How do you explain THAT to your wife or partner? Yeah, he was a bit too risky, but I liked taking risks; it added to the excitement and thrill.

He still became a bit of a regular at mine, usually coming round to my house for a session before he started work very early in the morning. No wonder I was so knackered! I had to get up early to shower and slap some make-up on to disguise the 'I look like death warmed up' look. But it made my day more enjoyable and I was more contented, shall we say. I would sit there at work, in my office at home, with a stupid knowing smile on my face, still answering the phones like a professional. If only people knew. That made it even funnier in my now twisted mind.

Things did become a little nervy between us when I went to the local cinema alone one night. I'd pre-booked a seat on the back row as it was the best vantage point in the small venue, plus it had a little more leg room. The staff member scanning my ticket at the back of the cinema began huffing and puffing as my ticket wouldn't scan from my iPhone. I also had a printed copy of the ticket, so I emptied my handbag contents out to find it. That wouldn't scan either! A heated discussion occurred, shall we say, with me telling him, 'That's not MY fault, it's your machine! Technology, and all that.' We ended up laughing about it, and I said for him not to evict me from my seat as I HAD paid for my ticket online. My big booming Hull accent becoming more prominent the more I was talking and laughing. All seemed okay, it was forgotten about, and I went to my seat with a slight grin on my face thinking about the member of staff, an old man, coming to evict me from my seat before the film began.

Unbeknown to me, Ian was already seated in that cinema and had heard the commotion and recognised my Hull accent. I didn't live in Hull anymore, so if I was anywhere else, my accent stuck out like a sore thumb. When I eventually got to my seat, he turned around and did a double take and just glared at me. I nearly fell out of my seat with shock, as I obviously hadn't expected him to be there, so just looked blankly at him. He was one row directly in front of me, sat with a woman, presumably his wife! Yes, the one who allegedly 'didn't want sex anymore'. If his wife saw any recognition, then she would be curious as to who I was. I didn't want, or need, any questions. I sat there poker-faced.

Unfortunately, I then had to spend the next two hours looking at the back of his head ... and hers! Listening to his false laughter during the film, and watching him try to put his arm around his wife in a loving gesture. Almost, I felt, to make me jealous. I didn't care. I wasn't married or having an affair, but he was. She was welcome to him. It was a cringeworthy display of misplaced affection, and I bet she was wondering why he was suddenly so loving towards her – if only she knew. It could have been worse, I told myself; imagine if I had to sit next to him, or his wife. I laughed to myself imagining being sat next to him in the cinema – he would be mortified and so scared. It would only take a few words from me and his whole world would come crashing down; his marriage, family and business – absolutely everything. I certainly didn't want him staying at my house with all his baggage, or his wife knocking at my door, questioning me. He knew deep down that I had power over him. I had the evidence from his sexy text messages to me, his dick pics, holiday photos and his fantasies, so he had better treat me bloody right. I was in control – not him.

He made contact the next week and came round to see me. 'God, I so wished you were sat next to me and put your hand on my leg in the cinema,' he gushed, like it was a turn-on for him. I smirked as I knew he would really have been shitting himself. It was bad enough at the end of the film when, as soon as the credits rolled, he almost pushed his wife out of her seat to exit the cinema – and fast. Yeah, he was bloody scared. He needn't have worried. I was hardly likely to go over to her and say something ridiculous such as, 'Hi, pleased to meet you. I am your husband's lover. We've been shagging for a few weeks now. Oh, and by the way, I had sex with him before he went to work yesterday morning.' She would either break down in tears or possibly slap me, hard, across my face. I wasn't here to break up any marriage or confess anything to any partner. Men had to respect me, and I would respect them. He still had a hell of a lot to learn.

CHAPTER 12

HUNGRY LIKE THE WOLF

He was young and blond-haired, with a super slim, sexy body, and the only passable, attractive bloke in the swingers' club that Sunday evening that I wanted sex with. He was young, dumb and full of cum. Actually, I may have been wrong; he was certainly young and full of cum. I wasn't yet sure about the dumb part. But two out of three ain't bad. I was sat at the bar in the club when I caught his eye and he smiled. I smirked to myself. I was like a cougar in stealth mode. He was my next prey, and he didn't even know it – yet!

I lifted myself off my bar stool and left my fuck buddy sitting all alone at the bar. I was now going in search of my prey. My fuck buddy was such a moody sod, and I had had enough of him sulking as he couldn't find a woman he liked. On a more positive note, my prey was now in sight, and I certainly wasn't going to let this one get away easily, if at all.

I decided that I would have a quick fuck, then go home. After all, it was nearly an hour's drive back home, and I had to get up early for work the next day. I really hadn't got time for small talk, and I was now tired. I wish I could say that I had better things to do at home, but that would be lying as I didn't. The more I stayed at home, the more I just cried with sadness and grief. I had tried so hard not to wallow in self-pity, but some days it was bloody hard. In fact, my whole life was bloody hard most days.

I found Andy (my named prey) in the corridor area of the club. He had a towel around his waist and I could now see close up his smooth, sexy chest. I had a revealing dark purple lacy Ann Summers outfit on, hidden underneath my white towel. Lacy outfits also hid my scars and flab well. Men didn't realise that; they just thought it was super sexy. Let them think that – I wasn't bothered.

I smiled at him, gently touched his arm and asked, 'Shall we go into a room?'

He replied, slightly taken aback at me being so forward, 'Er ... didn't you want to talk first or have a drink?'

I responded sharply, 'Do I heck, babe! I've not come here to make small talk.' I was brazen and sluttish, but I was beyond caring. Was he for fucking real? This was a bloody swingers' club – not a Starbucks or a Wetherspoons pub. If I'd wanted to make small talk and drink a frothy coffee or half a lager, I would have gone there. I looked him up and down. Yeah, he really WAS young, dumb and full of cum. Three out of three. But I needed to get home soon to get some sleep, and now time was ticking on. Let's get this bloody show on the road!

I found a small private room in the club for couples only, and we went in. I almost pushed him inside in case he changed his mind. I turned round and quickly bolted the door behind us so as not to be disturbed. He would be all mine for the next fifteen minutes or so, and no one else's. I had to make my journey to Leeds worthwhile and certainly wasn't going to leave until I had my money's worth.

I'm sure he wasn't disappointed; we took it in turns to please each other repeatedly. He looked shattered after we had finished our frenzied 'liaison' together. We both lay down, sweating and breathless, after slipping and sliding on the large plastic-coated bed, which was now dripping with our sweat. It was blooming hot in that room in more ways than one. We looked at each other seriously and both burst out laughing, giving each other a high-five, as if we had just competed in an Olympic relay race and won a gold medal. I knew one thing, and that was that I certainly liked his baton. But this was better than any medal. It was purely good sex, possibly on the verge of porn movie standard, and we both didn't care.

I had got my money's worth, and now this cougar could go home to have a catnap. Thanks, Andy, your cougar had caught her prey and was satisfied. A bit like the cat that got the cream.

CHAPTER 13

BLUE MONDAY

These dating apps and Tinder men were beginning to irritate me; they were becoming demanding – well, they could think again. Wanting to come round and visit me before and after work – as if I had nothing better to do. I was also getting fed up with the practical side of things, such as having to shave my legs daily, and obviously shave other areas, and having to apply full make-up and make my hair look presentable all the time. Never mind the outfits they wanted me to wear. It all took time and effort, which I was lacking most days, and they didn't even seem to appreciate it. I decided that things would have to change, and very soon. I was in charge, NOT them. This was MY house and MY rules.

Ian, one of my Tinder regulars (the cinema man), wanted to come round to 'see me' one Monday morning before I started work. I was still working from home and started work at eight o'clock. I told him that he had better be at mine blooming early that morning. I sent him a text message to remind him that he had to be early – or else.

I had slapped enough make-up on to warrant being an upper-class hooker; I had used the eyeshadow he liked – dark grey for the sultry, slutty look – and masses of mascara and black eyeliner. I knew I looked bloody good as I squeezed into a black leather-look basque that zipped up at the front and tied at the sides. Shoving my boobs upwards even higher, just to complete the slutty and hooker look.

Ian eventually turned up – late. I was absolutely fucking fuming. I had been standing at my front door, patiently waiting, literally freezing my tits off in that basque. 'You've now got less than twenty minutes, so you'd better make it bloody quick!' I bellowed at him as he came through the front door. Some men liked that. I couldn't care less if he did or he didn't. He deserved to be treated like a naughty child. He said he was sorry and blamed a work telephone call. I couldn't give a shit about the phone call, or that he was in charge of a multi-million pound company; he did as he was told in my house – I was in charge here. He wasn't at work giving the orders – I was. It was role reversal in my house for all of them.

I looked at him and sighed loudly with impatience as he took off his shoes in the hallway. We would now have to forgo the foreplay this morning as we didn't have time; he always got too excited too soon anyway and came quickly. We went upstairs and had a quick session in the spare bedroom. Anything was better than nothing, I supposed, to help get me through the day.

The time was now almost bloody eight o'clock. His time slot was over. I quickly got off the bed, went downstairs and stood half naked, holding my front door open for him to leave. I didn't care that I lived on a main road and traffic was at a standstill outside my house in the morning rush hour. I was still in my basque – which was now skew-whiff – my hair looked like I had been dragged through a hedge backwards, my eyeshadow was now creased and bright red lipstick was randomly smeared across my face from when I had kissed him bloody hard on his mouth and other areas of his body. Let everyone see who was sitting in the queue of traffic outside; it would give them something to talk about when they got to work. I just didn't care anymore.

'Blooming heck ... JUST GO!' I bellowed at him as he came down the stairs, still getting dressed. 'I need to be logged onto the helpdesk at work by eight!' He quickly put on his shoes. I watched him drive away in his large Mercedes car and slammed the front door shut. The flipping idiot. Now I hadn't time to have a wee, another shower, or even get dressed properly. It didn't really matter as no one could see me working from home, and on the phones. I would get changed at my first coffee break, in a couple of hours' time. I strutted barefoot on tiptoes, like a trotting horse, through the house and went into my office at home, still half naked. I logged onto work, still huffing and puffing to myself about his stupidity and lateness. I put my headset on and began my usual helpdesk shift.

I really hated Mondays, as unfortunately it was one of my boring helpdesk days. It was the busiest day of the week. Usually, servers had gone down, people had somehow forgotten their passwords over the two days that was the weekend (some people *really* had the memory of a bloody goldfish!), and systems weren't working as they should. I sighed to myself, anticipating yet another busy week of continual calls. In fact, every day now seemed like a helpdesk day to me. It drove me insane with boredom, but it paid my mortgage and bills so I couldn't, and shouldn't, really complain. My light relief, and special bonus today, was Ian. His quick session would help me get through this boring day. At least I was satisfied, but there was still room for improvement. I would have to tell him that next time.

A couple of hours passed, and I was due a break. Suddenly, just as I was about to log off to get changed into more suitable clothing, an internal work message popped up on my computer screen: *Emergency Teams meeting – please accept the request.*

HOLY SHIT AND FUCK! I wasn't exactly dressed for a Teams meeting in full view of everyone. I was more dressed for an OnlyFans private camming session. I grabbed a black silky dressing gown from the back of my office door, which was the only 'suitable' clothing I could find to hide my modesty and dignity. It was too small for me as it was for 'bedroom use only', and it didn't even cover much of my body, and certainly not my large cleavage, which was still pushed upwards towards the ceiling! I sat down and tried to hide my body from the head down by putting my office chair down a little bit and attempting to move my laptop a bit higher, so the camera didn't get a full view of me.

The meeting began and I'm sure that the other staff must have noticed something different. After all, I didn't usually wear a lot of make-up, if any. And I certainly didn't normally sit half-dressed on the helpdesk. Until today that is.

I heard my mobile phone beep on my desk. It was a text message from my work colleague, a male. I read it, dreading the content: *What the*

Fuck? Your cleavage is popping out and we can almost see your nipples. Have you just got in from a night out in Hull! And just look at your hair! It's like a cockatoo!

I quickly sent him a reply. *Bloody hell, no. Not been out on the town. I have been 'entertaining' but time was running out this morning and I need to get changed. I'm still in my shagging clothes. Not a cockatoo, only one cock!*

He replied, *Fucking hilarious, I've seen and heard it all now! It's like watching Babestation!*

I replied, *Thanks, mate, and you get this for free – I should be bloody charging you.* He sent a smiley face emoji to me, and we both tried to keep straight poker faces on the Teams meeting, staring at each other on screen, and possibly failing miserably.

Oh well, they do say that Team(s) work makes the dream work. I wasn't sure if this was a dream or a nightmare. Unfortunately, it was reality. I needed to get dressed – and bloody quick. Time to turn off that camera and take off my make-up, then continue my helpdesk day.

I made a mental note to give Ian some time management lessons next time I saw him. There was definitely 'room for improvement' in so many ways.

CHAPTER 14

ASHES TO ASHES

June 2022 was also another bad month; this was the norm now. It would have been Andrew's sixty-first birthday, if he was still here – a year later, which obviously he wasn't. Instead of his birthday celebrations, here I was, with a long list of things still to complete and now arranging for his headstone to be engraved and erected in the local cemetery. I tried to avoid going to the cemetery, and it took me days to get over the mental trauma of a visit. The last time I went there, I had even set another man off crying with my incessant sobbing at Andrew's grave. He was only there to visit his wife's grave and probably wanted peace and quiet. I ended up apologising to him, as he was perfectly okay – until he heard me. His sympathy and compassion just made me cry even more. 'Till death do us part' was so true in our case. I even began to think about the arguments Andrew and I previously had, to try and get a grip. Our relationship wasn't perfect; no relationship is. I knew I was trying to think of bad things so I wouldn't feel so upset! My head was seriously all over the fucking place.

Next on my traumatic long list of things to do was arranging Mother's cremation and the scattering of her ashes. She had died at Castle Hill Hospital a couple of weeks ago. My brother and I decided that there would be no funeral or any ceremony. She had no friends, so no one would even be there at her funeral. I had scoured the internet and found a cheap undertaker online, who dealt with cremations in the East Riding area. They were excellent and kept me informed every stage of the process. Unfortunately, they unknowingly rang me on my mobile phone whilst I was in the main office at work, on the bloody helpdesk. Advising me that the cremation would be on Friday at nine o'clock, in just a few days' time. I didn't know how I should feel. Sad? Happy? Remorseful? Glad she had finally gone? Who knew what I should be feeling? I certainly didn't know anymore. I now had to have time to think. This was it – the final farewell.

I walked calmly into the toilets at work and just cried; I didn't need this emotional shit. I was still working and trying to act professional through this entire mental trauma. I know my mother had hated me, the feeling was mutual, but she was still my mother, a person. Deep down, what really hurt was knowing that if the tables were turned and it was me that was dying, then she would not have gone to see me in hospital; she would have just let me die – alone. I needed to think clearly and remember that I DID see her when she was dying, as I had more compassion than she had ever had in her whole life.

Who in their right mind would let their daughter die alone? Well, I knew for a fact – SHE would. That thought sent me off into floods of tears yet again, as I knew deep down how much she had really hated me all my life. Who in their right mind would also walk out on their children for weeks, and let them fend for themselves when they were young and at primary school? Yes, SHE did. She had been so hateful and hurtful that it was beyond belief and my mental comprehension.

I just sat and had a good cry on the toilet; I didn't even need to use the toilet, but it was quiet in there. I tried to regain some composure and think positive thoughts, whatever they may be nowadays. Positivity was a rarity. I held my head high and walked back to my desk. I seriously couldn't give a shit if the other staff saw my red puffy eyes with my make-up now washed off from my big hot tears. I was sniffing and now counting down the minutes until I could leave at 4pm and get into my car to go home. Then I could cry and sob all I liked, to myself, on that forty-five-minute horrendous motorway journey home.

A week later, mother's ashes were delivered by post. I had to sign for them. I didn't even open the box; it remained in my porch until I decided when and where they would be scattered. She was certainly not coming into the house, our house. Andrew would haunt me if she even crossed the threshold into our house – DEAD OR ALIVE! She should count herself lucky she was even in the porch; she was only there as my shed was full of everyone's inherited crap that no one else wanted, and the box may have been thrown out by mistake into the local tip. She could now wait in MY cold, draughty porch until I was ready to scatter her in Hessle Cemetery. I was in control now, not her.

She had ruined my life since the day I was born. She had caused conflict between my brother and me, all our lives, the final nail in the coffin (pardon the pun) when she gave money to others and not me. Apparently their 'little family secret', never to be revealed. Well, I found out her secret by accident – over two years ago, resulting in a massive family argument and almost a physical fight. I was livid as she knew it would cause conflict, which is what she thrived on. I could hold my head up high and honestly say that everything I owned I had worked hard for, and had never been given a penny from her or my father (when he was alive). Stuff her fucking money. I had managed for this long without it. I didn't need it and made my own way in life – with or without money. I was a grafter, a hard worker in everything I did. She wasn't. She had inherited all her wealth from her mother and my father. I got nothing. The greedy cow. Stuff her.

Mother had hated every boyfriend I had when I was younger; Nick, Garry and Jeff. She hated Andrew and didn't even believe he was disabled, telling me he was lying and lazy. I didn't tell him, as he would have gone absolutely mad with her. Again, that is what she wanted – conflict and arguments. Then she would play the victim and sniff like she was crying. Andrew had called in many favours to help renovate her crappy run-down bungalow at 'mates' rates', ringing builders, TV aerial installers, carpet fitters, electricians, plumbers; everyone who could help. She never said thank you and appreciated nothing; it was almost expected behaviour that everyone would run around after HER.

I now looked at the sealed cardboard box in my porch with hatred and wished she had died before Andrew. How dare she even insult my husband, who would do anything for anyone? In fact, I wished she had died even before my father had, twenty-five years ago. She had probably nagged him to death after he took early retirement with ill health. If it wasn't for her, he would probably have had a quiet life in his last few years without being henpecked. Yes, Mother had even ground him down to being a weak man, having to obey her or his life would be hell; she would make sure of that. That narcissistic streak never left her. I had recently found photographs of my father in a photo album at the back of her wardrobe. Old black and white photos of him in Hamburg, Germany on National Service and in the Parachute Regiment, in a bar. Ironically, he looked happy with a tankard of beer in his hand, surrounded by his colleagues, all laughing. When I thought about it, I realised that I had never really seen him smiling or even heard him laughing. SHE had caused him to be like that – bloody miserable and sad.

It now took all my willpower not to take the cardboard box and throw it out of the porch and onto my driveway, or even over my fence onto the busy main road. In my mind, I imagined a car or lorry driving over the box, crushing it, and the ashes inside, HER ashes, spread all over the road. But that would mean that she would have the last laugh as she'd be outside my house, lingering and loitering.

I took a few deep breaths, slammed the front door shut and walked away into the other room to put the kettle on. I wasn't sure whether to have a coffee, a pint of cider or a gin and tonic, the way I was feeling at that precise time – I was seriously done with it all. As it was only ten o'clock in the morning, I decided on a coffee, a safer option the way I was feeling. Mother could wait. This was now MY house and MY rules.

CHAPTER 15

SWING WHEN YOU'RE WINNING

I switched on my computer and went online; the dating apps were still an addiction. They gave me escapism from the daily mental shit that was now my life.

I met Hot Tub Terry through a swingers' website that some people at the swingers' club recommended and used. His profile and details came up in the local area I searched. Best of all, he lived quite close to my house. According to his profile, he had a hot tub in his back garden. In these days of saving money, a hot tub session sounded quite nice as it saved me getting a bath and paying for water. A girl has to look at the practicality of these situations. After all, I was on a water meter and certainly couldn't afford to fill up my own bath with hot water.

Terry messaged me back, asking what I wanted from our 'meet-up'. I was brazen as I hadn't time for small talk anymore. My reply was to the point: *I want a dip in your hot tub, and a fuck.* Obviously, this seemed to entice and encourage him, and he asked me to come round. Shit, I really had gone too far this time. My sexual language was now a bit too full-on and explicit from all the chatlines talk. But 'nothing ventured, nothing gained', as they say. I went through with it. Going into his house, we had a drink and talked, then went into the hot tub. I was wearing a tankini to cover my large deep wonky scars still showing on my stomach. Afterwards, we went to his bedroom and we fucked like crazy. Why not? I was single, he was single – sort of.

He told me the news that he still had a fuck buddy. What The Fuck – literally! A young fuck buddy, yet he was on a swingers' website looking for more? Holy shit! I didn't know what to say. He then asked me, 'Oh, don't forget to add a verification on that swingers' website about me.' I looked at him, puzzled.

I was slightly bothered by the fact he had said that during lockdown the swingers' clubs were all closed, and he was bored. I was personally more concerned during lockdown with trying to keep my husband safe and alive by shielding us both, to save his life. Terry was on a totally different wavelength; we had different priorities. His was having sex; mine was trying to save a life.

When I got back home, I logged onto the website we had met through and again viewed his profile. Sure enough, there were loads of 'verifications' from other people about his 'performance' from the last few years. SHIT, I didn't see that before! It was like a Trustpilot review page, or 'Rate My Plate'. It was even beyond 'Rate My Date'. It was 'Rate My Sexual Performance', or 'How Big is Your Dick?' Every few weeks, someone had put some review of him on there. Sentences such as *We had arranged a gangbang and he did not disappoin*t and *My legs were like jelly and shaking by the time we had finished* were prevalent. I cringed as I read a write-up about myself that he had already put on there. It was complimentary, luckily, but I didn't know I was being judged and personally commented on for this sleazy swinging website. How far did this need to go? I could imagine that next the website would introduce giving marks out of a total of ten, like the Olympic Games – for performance, stamina, best blow job, tightest pussy, longest penis ... the list could go on. Jeeeez, I certainly had a lot to learn. Thank goodness I had given a false name on the website and there was no photo of my face.

I had really been stupid this time. I thought I was the shameless one asking for a fuck, whereas he was a hardened swinger and had numerous (possibly hundreds) of fucks AND a fuck buddy. Was there no end to his talents? I was confused. Wasn't she enough? This was a whole new level of swinging and I was only a 'swinging virgin', as Terry had jokingly called me. I was now caught up in another surreal world; I had lost my way, my mind and my morals.

I knew it would end badly and sadly, and it eventually did. We began to have nights out together, not proper dates, just friendship dates. After all, I hadn't physically been out with many men yet and it felt weird. I opened some of my heart to him, and showed him my whole new life that I had built up over the past few months. Taking him to comedy gigs, pubs and cocktail bars in Beverley that he had never been to. I stupidly let him into my life for a while; he met my friends and I met some of his.

We both knew the score ... that he still had a fuck buddy, but I was in a higher class of shagging level by also seeing rich, professional married men who treated me well. I was more about quality than quantity, whereas Terry was totally about quantity and fucked anyone. Who was I to judge? I wasn't there to judge anyone's lifestyle; I was as bad as he was. We seemed to do our own thing but came together for dates and sex. It was a combination that worked, and we both knew the score.

All was going okay with this arrangement, until he was due to come round to my house one night after work, and we were going to telephone out for a takeaway. He was late. I waited half an hour before I texted him, Is everything okay?

His response being very short and sharp: *I am not in the mood for a takeaway. I have had an argument with a friend, and I do not feel like it.*

Well, that is bloody brilliant, I thought. He could have let me know earlier. I had been at work, rushed to get ready, slapped some make-up on and tidied the house the best I could, and was hungry as I was waiting to see what he wanted to eat. I didn't know who was the bigger idiot – me or him. I found out later that the argument had been with his fuck buddy, yeah, his so-called 'friend'.

A week later, he messaged me, asking me to come round to his house. I went round, thinking he genuinely wanted to see me, and maybe even apologise. Unfortunately, I was wrong. I went to his house, and he shouted me to come in and then called down the stairs to me to bring up a beer from his fridge, if I wanted one. He was already in his bed, the bedroom in darkness as the curtains were closed. He was drinking a can of beer; the bedroom bin was already overflowing with empty beer cans. We talked briefly as I got undressed to my underwear and got into his bed. He said he wasn't upset about his fuck buddy anymore. Well, he could have bloody fooled me, drinking and sulking, yet he wasn't upset? He told me things about her that I didn't want to, or need to, know. I suddenly felt awkward and uneasy, almost as if I was intruding in their relationship.

I chose a comedy film on Netflix. We laughed as we watched it, and we fucked. That's all it seemed to be – Netflix and fuck. We had a powerful, urgent, long sex session. But a fuck with no real emotion anymore. The connection we had, had gone. I knew we were over. I obviously wasn't good enough for him; no woman would ever be. I wasn't there just to feed his sex addiction; I had genuinely just wanted his trust and friendship, not just a fuck. I was as much to blame with my brazen comment *A dip in your hot tub and a fuck ...*

I had foolishly let him into my life. This had all backfired. My invisible barriers would be up once again, never to come down. I walked away. I was emotionally hurt. After all, I may be a swinger but was certainly not a minger. I had more respect for myself. Even though that was debatable at times.

CHAPTER 16

LEARNING TO FLY
(BUT I AIN'T GOT WINGS)

Here I was, spending all my inheritance money in advance. Now on board Emirates flight EK18X from Manchester to Dubai just a few weeks after Mother had died. I sat at the window seat of the plane, almost in an act of rebellion, defiance and revolt, staring out at the runway at Manchester Airport. Their advert stated 'Fly Emirates, Fly Better'. That's okay, as I would certainly be doing that.

'Yes, please,' I replied when Emirates asked if I would like any of the extras on board the flight; additional leg room, fast track at the airport, etc. I would have it all, thank you. Unfortunately, I couldn't quite justify First Class or Business Class, such as I was used to with Andrew. But this was a flipping good start. In Dubai, I had booked a big family hotel suite, not a hotel room, in one of the most exclusive hotels, with a sea view, right on the beachfront at Jumeirah Beach Residence, which also had a private beach. I would be eating lobster and drinking champagne at the Hilton in their best restaurant, whatever the cost. This was MY life and MY time, and the next two weeks were going to be amazing.

My mother was always 'as tight as a duck's arse', as Andrew used to say to me. He was right. She had never ever given me a penny in the whole of my life. She had seen me homeless and destitute and she had loved it; in fact, she actually thrived on it. I was always the 'black sheep of the family'. I would never ever forget her vindictiveness and spitefulness towards me.

I would also never forget that just before my horrendous divorce over twenty years ago, she had slapped my young son, hard, right across his face, and even admitted it. He was crying, looking at me afterwards, with a bright red hand mark across his cheek – HER hand mark. She was bloody sneaky and had done it in another room so I wasn't there, and she was out of view. She couldn't, and didn't, even deny it.

I was devastated and shocked as I had never been violent to my son. He was also shocked and confused by the ferocity and randomness of the slap. Her continual pattern of abuse had now escalated to my son, HER grandson, almost like it was hereditary and HAD to be done – you know, 'keep it in the family'. Keep the child frightened and scared. She was a bitch of a witch and would never change. Her mental health was beyond any help, in my opinion. My father had once put it down to 'her nerves'. Yeah, well, she got on everyone's bloody nerves, for all the wrong reasons.

I remember screaming at her like a crazed banshee, shrieking at the top of my voice. I was hysterical; my son was now crying even more. What the fuck was she thinking of? Why the fuck had I even brought my son to see her? I had only done it out of politeness as people were judging me. 'Blood is thicker than water,' they would say, and all that crap. Well, take some bloody warfarin or blood thinners then, if your blood is too thick. This was no normal family; it was violent and dysfunctional. I thought Mother might have mellowed in her old age. Well, obviously not. The old, bitter, twisted bitch from hell.

Now this drama with the slap across the face had allowed authorities and bloody social services to get involved. My fucking secret dread during messy divorce proceedings, and I was right to be worried. The end result, after being dragged through numerous upsetting court hearings in Hull and a ridiculously inaccurate CAFCASS report, was that I lost custody of my son, and he went to live with my now ex-husband. Allegedly to live in a 'safer environment'.

It fucking sickened me to the stomach. He was no better than she was, despite what the court reports said! I was suddenly made out to be a bad, uncaring mother, which was untrue and unfair. I had taken my son away from domestic violence and put myself in the firing line. I took the rap for it all – to protect my son. The court didn't see it that way and said that as there was no history of bruises on my son, then there was no evidence he was in danger. No, the blinkered idiots! The bruises were on ME, and I had my doctor's reports to prove it, along with other professionals' reports. I was amazed, and to this day I am still shocked, at that outcome from the courts. Mother, and my ex, were both bloody good masters of disguise and could pull the wool over everyone's eyes. I don't ever forgive and certainly would NEVER EVER fucking forget.

This whole drama had ruined my life and my future. I had sent a letter all those years ago to CAFCASS, anonymously. Sarcastically thanking them for their blinkered outlook and for ruining my life. I didn't care who read it. It was true. I knew it would have just been screwed up and thrown in their wastepaper or recycle bin – but my point had been made. I even wrote in that letter that I wasn't sure how they could sleep at night – as I certainly couldn't ... without MY son. I had lost everything in an instant; my child, my expensive detached house, all my possessions – because of HER! People wondered why I then tried to commit suicide by taking an overdose. Well, that was the reason. HER, my mother – along with our legal system. I have no shame and will admit that.

SHIT! I quickly shook my head, coming out of my trance-like state. I had to get a fucking grip. This was not the time to lose my nerve and reminisce during a long-haul flight. We were still on the bloody runway at Manchester Airport and had not even taken off yet! *Not to worry*, I told myself silently, trying to reassure myself. *That is all behind me in my past life, it happened many years ago. This is now my future.* I certainly wouldn't forget this luxurious holiday in a hurry. I deserved this and would make the most of it. I would be frivolous and free for the first time in my life and would bloody well embrace it.

Yes, I had many regrets. Mainly, I regretted that my mother hadn't died before my beloved husband, Andrew – then we BOTH could have enjoyed her money. We BOTH deserved it, as she didn't even believe he was disabled. She had loved to tell me that he was 'a waste of space' and sarcastically tell me, 'I don't know why you even married him.'

Well, Mother – I married him because I loved him, in sickness and in health and all that. But don't worry, as here I am, enjoying YOUR money and living the high life. I may unfortunately be without my husband, but I am making the most of my life alone – more than YOU ever did. Let me raise a glass of champagne to you in defiance and hatred, then raise a glass to my late husband with forever love. Fucking cheers, Mother.

CHAPTER 17

OUT OF MY DEPTH

Moses was younger than me by about thirty years. He worked at Dubai Aquarium within the luxurious, expensive Dubai shopping mall. His job was to assist and talk to tourists about the marine life in the aquarium, and also help direct people to the queue for the glass-bottom boat. I was in that queue of people, in Dubai. Alone. I had to wear a life jacket to go onto the boat. The aquarium depth was about 20 metres, not exactly a depth I would care to fall into without a life jacket.

Moses was there, as large as life, smiling falsely, his bright white teeth gleaming against his dark skin as he was handing out life jackets to the queuing tourists, also known as 'the unsuspecting public'. I looked a bit obvious as a 'single, blonde, busty, white female' in a queue full of families and couples. He suddenly homed in on me, as I guessed – no, I actually KNEW – he would do. 'You alone?' he asked outright.

'Yep,' I replied. I had now learnt to reply in one-word answers. It kept people guessing and saved me from speaking too much when I couldn't be arsed.

'Ooh, are you from England? London?' he asked. I smiled falsely. The moment you mention England, people presume you live in London. I didn't correct him. My head was telling me that this conversation was starting in a direction I didn't really want it to, but I also wanted some entertainment and playtime on my two-week holiday, so carried it on. Let him think I was interested, and from London, when nothing could actually be further from the truth. If he wanted to play his flirty games, he was in luck; I was quite looking forward to his false flattery. I knew I was no great catch, unlike the expensive fish in that aquarium.

I knew his type, just out for what they can get from a tourist; sex, marriage, money and a UK visa or citizenship – I had heard it all before in the past year, and it was now bloody boring. Funnily enough, no bloke would have even spoken to me, or looked twice, if I was with Andrew. Now men gave me their full attention, unfortunately, and I would then be accused of not having any intention. Well, they got that correct then. As I certainly had NO intention. The idiots! They start it and then can't handle rejection. I could see right through their sleaze and money-grabbing banter. So yet again, here was another one right in front of me, to add to my constant growing list of losers. They were all like bees around a honey pot. Well, I was the queen bee, so they had all better bloody watch out.

Moses was trying to act professional and still holding out a life jacket for me. I put it on, and he proceeded to fasten the straps across the front of my chest, both his hands lingering a bit too much on my double D-sized breasts. I only had a thin 'Matalan special' summer dress on, as it was absolutely boiling hot in Dubai in June. At over 40 degrees outside, I was bloody sweating, to say the least. He would definitely be able to feel my bra and breasts beneath the thin material. He was such a flipping fool; I already knew how to fasten a life jacket as I used to help out at Humber Rescue in Hessle. I would let him think I was a bit naïve and would play his little game. I hoped he enjoyed his free grope. I gave him an insincere smile. I didn't need him, but I knew from that moment that HE needed me.

As soon as the boat ride had finished, he was right there. Grinning like a fool at the end of the floating platform, taking off my life jacket then quickly ushering me into the large glass aquarium area to show me the fish and crocodiles. When he showed me the sturgeon in the large glass tank, I made the mistake of opening my mouth. 'Yeah, they're cool, we used to have some of those in our pond at home.' Shit. I should have kept quiet. He immediately cottoned on to this comment, I noticed. He began asking where in London I lived, and then randomly pointing out that on his work's name badge it showed the Union Jack flag along with the flag of Ghana. As if I was actually interested. I wasn't.

As we walked around the aquarium, he told me that his ambition was to get a job in England. *Here we go ...* I thought. Moses said he had a house that was half finished in Ghana. He only needed £15,000 to complete it, hence wanting to work in London to earn more money to finish the house. I smirked sarcastically and nodded slowly, knowingly. I would now let him do all the talking, as he would obviously say the same thing to every single woman who he thought he could con some money out of. This was now free additional entertainment on my holiday.

He was slick, I will give him that. Producing his mobile phone out of his pocket and showing me photos of a large half-built breeze block construction detached house, which was allegedly his. Telling me what a good life it was in Ghana, where I could apparently 'wake up with the wildlife'. I don't know where he got the idea of me even going over there from. I certainly didn't even want to wake up with him, OR any of the wildlife in Ghana. I had never even wanted to go on a safari, as I was a city girl at heart. Moses' photos of his fictitious house were lovely. He was talking too fast and gibberish and I knew he was lying. I just let him carry on with his waffling patter and chatter. He looked at me and said he felt nervous and embarrassed. Yeah, he should be ashamed and embarrassed, for chatting up a woman old enough to be his mother. He was obviously desperate for money and a visa.

He took a couple of photographs of us both at the aquarium, and I made another mistake of giving him my mobile number so he could send them to me. Oh well, I could block him if he became a pest. This would certainly be the case, and he would be blocked – very soon.

Moses asked where I was staying in Dubai. I noticed his eyebrows raised and his eyes got wider when I mentioned the hotel on The Walk at Jumeirah Beach Residence. I didn't tell him I paid for it from my mother's inheritance – it was MY treat and MY business.

Moses said he would like to come and see me at the hotel, not seeming to care that this behaviour would be frowned upon in Dubai and its culture. I laughed as I certainly didn't care; I didn't live over there, but

HE did. He could be an 'additional extra' to my holiday, yes, a free additional extra. I like freebies.

He came to see me one morning, knocking quietly at my hotel door and rushing into my room as soon as I opened it. Telling me he hoped that no one, especially the police, had seen him. So much for the bravery he had shown at the aquarium. Now he was running scared, literally. I looked at him and sighed, not with affection but with exasperation. We had straight sex. I could tell he had no experience; he probably thought he was being mature buying some condoms en route. Goodness knows why he had bought a large packet, as one condom would be more than enough, the way I was feeling at that precise time.

I quickly went into the bathroom in my hotel suite. When I came out, I found Moses opening the cupboards in the room and eating some mints I had put away in the drawer. 'OKAY – what the HELL is going on?' I almost shouted at him.

'No, no, no, you can't swear or shout in Dubai. It's against the law,' he replied patronisingly, and with a little aggression.

I quickly responded, 'YOU probably shouldn't have had pre-marital sex in Dubai either. IT'S against the law – but YOU have.' He pretended not to be that bothered, but I could tell I had rattled and annoyed him. I felt the conversation was now on dodgy ground and was getting slightly worried for my safety.

He swiftly changed the subject from him rummaging about in my cupboards in the room, and randomly mentioned that my Nike backpack, which was on the floor, was expensive. I replied that yes it was, obviously not telling him it was on special offer from Sports Direct in Hull. This conversation was suddenly getting very weird, and so was he. I was glad my possessions such as passport and credit cards were locked in the safety deposit box inside the wardrobe. I wasn't sure what he was angling at. Was he hoping I would give my backpack to him? Well, he could think again. 'Look, I really think you should go now, just in case the police DO find out, and also the housekeepers will be here soon to clean the room,' I said. I was suddenly feeling vulnerable and stupid at being so reckless with this stranger. He luckily left the hotel room. The housekeepers then knocked on the door and entered the room, thank goodness.

Unfortunately, Moses didn't forget me, and sent me the photos of us both at the aquarium, as promised. He contacted me again when I got back to England. His text messages were pathetic and needy, sometimes sending me several messages a day. *Babe, I miss you so much ... When are you coming back over to see me again? ... Please look out for jobs for me in London, try and get me a visa ..., I'm only on 10 dirhams an hour, I need to eat ... I have no money left this month.* I had heard it all before. Moses would probably do this to all the single female tourists he met. He had his own personal 'Aquarium Tinder'. His pathetic begging was beginning to sound like Loy, the oil rig worker. It was all like déjà vu. Let's add the 'Garage Tinder' into the mix whilst we are at it. These men must read from the same book of desperation and pitiful phrases. All looking for the 'phrase that pays'.

They were using their employment status to their advantage, for dating or scamming innocent people. They presumed it was 'perks of the job'. Did they seriously think I was naïve and didn't know their hidden agendas and mind games? Give it up, Moses. We had rubbish sex, and then you thought I would give you money. Really?

Moses, you are blocked and deleted. You are like a fish out of water in your large aquarium and in my life.

CHAPTER 18

CURIOSITY KILLED THE CAT

Before I begin this chapter, I will just mention one thing. I am totally straight, not even a bit bi-curious until someone made me doubt myself. If I was going to even contemplate having a relationship with a woman, she would have to be like myself: tall, busty and curvy, and also a bit of a confident loudmouth. Let's just say that I am now a more assertive person and take no prisoners in this journey called life. I try not to have any regrets in my life, only experiences.

I wasn't into sharing in the bedroom. I was, and still am, a one-on-one person – even at the swingers' club. Mechanic Boy convinced me, months ago, that it was 'normal' to share nowadays. He'd been to another couple's house that had a hot tub, to share each other (as in swinging), as if it was something normal. But admitted he didn't even have sex. He was left out, though, whilst others enjoyed themselves – what the heck? I personally didn't think it was for me, especially if I was in a relationship, but everyone is different and has different fantasies. I was more fascinated about the principle of why people did it. Why they swapped partners. I became more and more intrigued. Mechanic Boy encouraging me all the time, I admit I felt under pressure, even thinking I might be missing out. The conclusion to this is that I was bloody wrong and should have trusted my initial instincts and not gone ahead.

I put myself onto a swingers' website as a 'unicorn' as a bit of a joke. For those that don't know, the definition of a 'unicorn' in a normal dictionary is *'a mythical animal resembling a horse or a goat, with a single horn on its head'.*

However, the definition in Urban Dictionary is very different: *'a common swinging term used in the community to refer to a single female interested in meeting other couples. A rare treat'.*

I think the Urban Dictionary meaning won in my case. I was a 'rare treat'.

A married couple made contact with me very soon after my profile went on the website. They were from the Leeds area, and we exchanged photographs online and a bit of background information of what we were all looking for. She was a small, petite, dark-haired lady. He was tall and a bit skinny, and said he liked the 'natural look'. He was in for a shock then, as I now had Botox regularly pumped into my face and had a breast reduction many years ago. I certainly didn't have the natural unshaven look he was apparently looking for and loved so much. I told him this truthful information about myself; he didn't seem put off or repulsed by it – after all, they had to play by my rules if they wanted the rare treat of a unicorn.

We met at a café on the outskirts of Leeds, a nice select area, and all sat outside in the warm July sun, drinking frothy coffee and chatting about our jobs. After an hour of talking, we all went back to their house. We continued to talk in the front living room and the lady said she used to be in the care sector. I could tell, as she was genuinely kind. Unlike myself, who had suddenly turned into a hard, aggressive bitch. We were personalities apart. I got the feeling this was his idea, not hers. Mainly as it was her that set the boundaries and rules about what was acceptable, and what wasn't, to them both in the bedroom. But apparently the rules may change as things progressed. I looked in disbelief but let her carry on as if she was in charge. When, really, it was ME that was in charge. Didn't they realise that? Obviously not.

The rules were relayed to me almost like being at school. There was to be no kissing or touching of any area below the waist of her husband, but he could touch me on my boobs, but not have sex. They had to build up to sex with me over the next few weeks if we all got on together. Bloody hell, I thought, I could be at the swingers' club now in Leeds, actually having full-on penetrative sex, rather than here, at the house of a couple of strangers, making small talk about what was and wasn't acceptable. Little did they know that I don't abide by rules.

I was thinking to myself – *So why AM I here then?* But I WAS there. I had travelled all the way to the other side of Leeds, so I might as well go with the flow. But this had better be bloody good; otherwise, I had wasted my time AND petrol. It was still sunny outside and I had better places to be than sat in their front room being polite by drinking another cup of coffee, listening to her random rule book and also having their cats jumping onto me like I was a bloody springboard.

The truth was that I didn't even fancy him or her. I didn't have the 'I wanna rip your clothes off and shag you so bloody much' fluttering feeling in my stomach that I had felt before with some men, even at the swingers' clubs.

I tried to act confident, like this was second nature, a common occurrence in my life. Secretly, inside, I was cringing – they were lovely people and admitted they'd never shared before. Would I upset the dynamics of their strong marriage? I wasn't here to destroy anyone's relationship. They hadn't even been into a swingers' club before, and they were both new to it all. I was their first and they were MY first couple – and I was certain that they would be my last! I would have felt more comfortable actually in the sweaty swingers' club with plastic beds. Not now in someone's front bedroom that had a flowery duvet, flowery wallpaper and an old-style chest of drawers in the corner. I felt I was intruding in their private space and place but remembered that they knowingly put themselves out there on THAT website.

I really wanted to go leave, go home, but also felt a strong compulsion, and strange curiosity, to stay. I should have faked an illness or something and just left. I certainly wasn't bi-sexual and had never had any bi-curious tendencies. I liked men too much, I admit it. But I wasn't even getting sex by the sound of it that morning.

They stripped off totally naked. I kept my panties on for the time being. I don't know why, but I suddenly felt a bit embarrassed. Not many people had seen me naked in the daylight, or even at all, until the last few months. She had smaller breasts than myself, and they both said that my breasts looked amazing. My breasts had been reduced in size and lifted higher, so would never droop down like Spaniel's ears, like some women's had. I knew they looked good as loads of blokes at the swingers' club commented and thought I had had implants ... I hadn't, they were natural. Naturally reduced! Funnily enough, I had never even thought my boobs looked any different to any other women's. But apparently they do, as men were quick to tell me in the club. I just accepted it as a compliment, and if I knew who the surgeon was some twenty years previous, I would personally thank him a hundred times over.

Her husband put some bath towels on top of their bed. They weren't even matching towels and had seen better days; they were a bit threadbare. In fact, I had thrown better towels away in my wheelie bin. I tried not to think about it. Maybe I was just too choosy and had higher standards. Maybe I was just a snob. One of my ex-boyfriends had once called me a stuck-up snob, not that I believed him. There was nothing wrong with having higher standards and values – in my opinion.

Seeing her laid on the bed on her back, with a big black hairy bush on show, turned me off even more. I wanted to run out of the door but didn't want to appear rude. He looked at me and said, 'I just love the natural look, unshaven. It's like being in a porn film.' I smiled out of politeness, as of course he loved his wife, shaved or not. It seemed to be his choice for his wife to have a hairy pussy along with a hairy backside.

Yes, I thought, *like a bloody porn film from the 1970s, when shaving wasn't popular and nearly everyone had a big hairy bush.* In my mind, I could imagine it was like going through the undergrowth of a jungle. He needed to get to the club in Leeds and watch the current porn films there – not a pubic hair in sight. Or get to Pulse & Cocktails on the A63 into Hull, plenty of porn DVDs there with no hairy bushes on the front covers. I kept quiet as I was now actually unsure why I was even there.

They had sex in front of me whilst I watched; bored, listening to her amateur, almost silent, orgasm and hoping he would cum very soon. They were both really quiet at having sex. Maybe it was just me that was noisy and shouty, I thought. Well, at least I put a lot more effort into it, almost an athletic standard. But that was me. I liked to be a good participant rather than a spectator in all things, including sport and sex.

Put it like this, my bed bloody shook when I was having good sex. It was like an exciting white-knuckle ride at Alton Towers. The headboard banging like crazy into the wall and denting it, bed sheets gripped onto tightly – almost being ripped, bodily fluids all over the bed, then the gasping and shouting of exhilaration and orgasm. And then why not throw in a legs-apart fanny fart to finish it all off! Yeah, that was MY definition of sex nowadays!

But unfortunately … not today. Not here, in front of me – their mattress hardly even moved. THEY hardly moved. I certainly wasn't bloody moved. It was like sex in slow motion. A bit like those wildlife programmes on the television when two tortoises are mating, and they look static, almost dead. The kind of situation where you just want to poke them gently with a stick, to see if they move and are still alive. I sighed quietly. Maybe it was just me that had more enthusiasm then. Possibly bordering on pornographic levels at times. I didn't care. I had no complaints from any of my men, along with no inhibitions.

She had already stated 'no touching'. But when she was in a doggy position on the bed, facing the aged faded Dralon headboard, her hairy asshole in the air, he had secretly put his hand on my pussy and his fingers inside me and looked at me with a smirk on his face. I just knew he couldn't resist a shaved pussy. I winked at him – and then shoved his fingers even higher. That was my part of the fun, my power over them both. He had broken his own wife's set of rules, and she had no idea. I had no rules and no morals, I just didn't care.

I was now knelt up on their bed, naked and bored. I could see out of their bedroom window, as the curtains were half open, looking at the smartly cut front lawns opposite with rose bushes as borders. I began daydreaming about tortoises. Not many people had them nowadays compared to when I was younger in the 1970s. Then there was that tortoise on *Blue Peter*, and one on *Pipkins*. I don't think there was one on *Tales of the Riverbank* – that was mainly hamsters and guinea pigs ... This was now a fucking nightmare; I wanted to leave. Why was I now thinking about tortoises whilst watching two people having sex? Oh yes, because I was bloody bored! She changed position and clambered on top of him, and he eventually ejaculated, thank goodness. He still had one hand on one of my boobs, so I daren't move. After he came, I quickly got dressed and waited downstairs. Their cats were now going crazy and jumping all over the furniture in the living room.

I was wishing they'd hurry up and come downstairs. Just how long does it take to get bloody dressed? Personally, I was quick at getting dressed and undressed. It came naturally with months of practice ... After all, it doesn't take long to get dressed, and literally a few seconds for me to get undressed, especially if good sex was about to happen. Everything would be off in a flash, clothes abandoned on the floor. Unfortunately, this hadn't been one of those days.

The cats were now a bit calmer, sitting on the front bay window sill. One was black and reminded me of her bush – black, spiky and hairy. Even the cats seemed to be waiting for my departure, almost telling me to 'fuck off'! I stared them out. I couldn't get away quickly enough. We all eventually said our awkward goodbyes and hugged in the front living room. They were lovely genuine people, but I knew it was a big mistake – his fantasy, and my curiosity – never again. There again at least he had seen and touched a shaved pussy. I reckoned he would be asking her to shave hers now. I have to think positive with every experience I encounter.

I went outside to my car. One of their neighbours had managed to almost block my bloody car in. I had a large estate car and had parked it outside their house near the end of the nice quiet cul-de-sac. Shit. I certainly wasn't going to go back into their house and ask which neighbour the car belonged to. The whole area had nicely manicured gardens with no fences, only rose bushes as a sort of boundary line. I've always hated rose bushes; bloody prickly, thorny horrible things.

Unfortunately, the nicely trimmed manicured garden opposite their house soon had my wide car tyre tread marks across them in my desperate attempt to leave in a hurry. I'd given up on my three-point turn in the tight area; there was only one way forward – and that was across the grass and over the thorny rose bushes. Yes, I left my mark all right, or rather the car did.

There are so many morals to this story ... 'A bird in the hand is worth two in the bush' springs to mind.

CHAPTER 19

WALK ON THE WILD SIDE

A few days later, I came across Dannii's photo on the same swingers' website. Dannii was a cross dresser, there was no mistake about that, but looked absolutely amazing. Her outfits were stunning, and so was she. I didn't even want sex – even though we were both now messaging each other. She had long blonde hair, dark eyes, and dressed in outfits so tight that her false boobs were hanging out. I could tell she was brazen and confident, and I bloody loved that. I love confident men and women and all they represent. There's a fine line between confident and arrogant, and SHE was definitely confident.

We arranged to meet at her place; she said she would be dressed as a woman. I asked her to send me a photo of her without any make-up on, as if she was going into work. She did; she looked even more gorgeous as a man. Dannii said that she had been out dressed as a woman in tight outfits to many events and concerts, and felt comfortable in high heels. I said that even I couldn't wear high heels without falling over, so all respect to her. I had already asked if, as a man, he was straight. He said he was, but just loved dressing up as a woman. I instantly had respect and admiration for him and his honesty.

Dannii wore a baby pink and white striped miniskirt outfit, with false boobs with pokey out nipples, and a gorgeous curly blonde wig when I visited her house. The house was immaculate, as I guessed it would be. A converted old building and very private. It was much tidier than mine – and I'm a woman who is supposed to enjoy tidying up and cleaning! The reality was that I bloody hated doing housework.

She had greeted me at her front door with a smile, her red lipstick just a bit too red and over the top, but I didn't care. I just looked into those large seductive eyes, knowing this was going to be something else. She, and he, was bloody gorgeous. I bit my bottom lip with anticipation and excitement; this was going to be a different sexual level and experience altogether.

We had a drink in the kitchen; she was knocking back some alcoholic spirits and admitted she was almost pissed from worry and apprehension of our meeting. She couldn't even walk straight. I wasn't sure if it was the pink high-heeled sandals she was wearing or the alcohol. I giggled like a silly schoolgirl, as I wasn't sure if I should laugh or help her. I had an orange juice as I was driving, and I needed to keep my wits about me. We had general chit-chat, talking about work and family. The family conversation was a bit one-sided, as I didn't really have any family as such. But there were no awkward silences. I did confess about the weekend before and the so-called threesome.

Dannii looked seriously at me and said I shouldn't have gone through with it. I admitted that I didn't have sex, but I was uncomfortable there. She stared into my eyes so much that it scared me but also mesmerised me, and said with determination, 'Always walk away if you feel uncomfortable and NEVER EVER do anything you don't want to do.' SHIT, that told me all right! But I knew she was right; I should have walked away, just like I should have walked away from so many other scenarios and situations in my life. I had to get real and try to show as much confidence as she did. Those words stuck in my mind and always will do. It was like she had almost brainwashed me into believing I was better than I thought I was, and I should tell people if I wasn't happy, and the reasons why.

Little did I know that by the end of that year I would have the determination and principles, like her, to do that. To actually tell my employer that I had had enough of their unrealistic expectations and demands, and quit my job. Bollocks to them. I learnt that it was quite liberating telling people your feelings and thoughts, especially in uncomfortable situations. For that, I will be ever grateful to Dannii and her words of wisdom. I was in awe of her intelligence, beauty and honesty.

We both went upstairs to her bedroom. Dannii had a huge wooden four-poster bed which had a 'dressing up box' underneath; it had lovely lacy outfits and bondage gear inside it. 'Babe, I am going to get changed into something more comfortable,' she said. 'Do you want to wait upstairs for me in another room?' I said I would, and made my way up the stairs to the top floor of her house, to get changed into my tight black PVC outfit. The room had amazing views of the countryside and rolling hills as I looked out of the small windows. There was a massive expensive full-length mirror, and I noticed that on the low ceiling beams there were hooks and a rope, along with handcuffs, carabiners and spreader bars. Shit, I certainly wouldn't be using the spreader bar ... anything could happen.

Dannii came up the stairs, in even higher heels, this time in black strappy sandals. God knows how she got up those stairs with those high heels on, but she did. She had a different wig on, now platinum blonde, wore black tights and a short black leather mini skirt, with a nice black frilly blouse. Her large false boobs took over her whole body and she loved it, and so did I.

We did bondage, and a photo shoot, which we both consented to. No naked photos, though. Laughing when we both nearly came into some difficulty when my wrists were tied wide apart to the low beams on the ceiling, and I was on my knees. When she went over to her camera on a tripod to set the timer and managed to trip over a tripod leg, stumbling and breaking her sandal strap, therefore nearly falling right on top of me. Of course, I couldn't move as I was tied up with both arms spread wide above my head, hands strapped in cuffs. Luckily, she regained her balance, even though she now had a broken sandal! In my mind, I was thinking how the hell would I be able to call any emergency services if she had fallen and hurt herself? Or even fallen on top of me. I would be stuck there, trussed up and tied up. She could be on the floor, with worse than a broken sandal, possibly even a broken leg! It would have been like a bondage comedy sketch that no one would have ever believed.

Dannii and I parted on good terms; we both got what we wanted out of our liaison and were happy. Dannii, you are an inspiration and aspiration that I will never forget.

The moral of the story is – 'during bondage, always have a safe word, and always wear safe shoes ... Not 6-inch high-heeled strappy sandals!'

CHAPTER 20

WANK HOLIDAY WEEKEND

It was bank holiday weekend at the end of August. I had nothing planned and was bored. Not like the Easter bank holiday, an amazing shag-fest when I received numerous Easter eggs from my 'men'. Danny even bought me two, along with his young sexy body. Or the excessive Jubilee bank holiday weekend in June, which was more like a jamboree than Jubilee celebrations in my house.

I was looking for something different to do and saw a local advertisement online for a three-course meal offer at Napoleon's Casino in Hull. The price also included a free bet and drink. *Why not?* I thought. Really random, but I hadn't been to a casino for over thirty years. I drove into Hull, entered the casino and filled in the membership form. I went upstairs and watched others gamble at the roulette wheel and had a couple of soft drinks. It was quite peaceful, to be honest, and I felt safe and comfortable.

My ex-husband had been a bit of a gambler, and I always swore I would never gamble. So, I didn't. I didn't really feel hungry enough to eat a three-course meal, and after a couple of hours, a bit of talking to people and more soft drinks, I was getting tired. I left the casino and walked back to my car, alone. After all, I hadn't gone there to pull a man; I just needed a change of scenery. Inside my car I swapped my high-heeled sandals for something a bit lower and more suitable for driving.

I glanced across the road from the casino car park. Just thirty seconds' walk away was HU9, the swingers' club; I swear it was beckoning me. I tried to resist going over that road to the club, I really did. But my willpower was zero and I knew that the night was still young; after all, it was bank holiday, and I had to enjoy myself.

I drove my car across the road to the side of the club as I knew the entrance was via the back door (if you pardon the pun). I put my high heels back on. Men were erecting (sorry!) an outside stage ready for the club's weekend activities. One of the men working on the stage shouted out to me, 'Don't worry, love, we ARE still open. Just push the door.' Shit, I was definitely committed now. It was too late to turn back; I would look foolish. I rang the buzzer and pushed open the heavy black door and entered the club. Disappointingly, it was almost empty. There was a young bloke at the bar, talking to a younger lady. They then both went to play a game of pool in the main bar area. I ordered a drink and had a wander upstairs to the playrooms; they were empty. I came back downstairs and sat down near the pool table but kept my distance from the other couple to give them privacy.

I felt a bit of a loner. I couldn't even play or text on my mobile phone, as no mobile phones were allowed in the club. All I could do was watch the porn on the large television screen near the bar. I was bored but tried to look interested. Telling myself I would give it two minutes, then that was it, I would leave. I was tired and still had to drive home.

Suddenly a bloke came in through the door – fresh blood! He was younger than me and I became very interested and, funnily enough, suddenly became wide awake. Almost acting like a meerkat, sat bolt upright and my eyes wide open. I could tell he hadn't been to the club before as the man behind the bar began speaking to him, and then escorted him to the ground floor area to show him around. Then they both walked by me to go up the metal staircase, presumably to view the playrooms and bondage chamber on the first floor. They came back downstairs and over to the bar area. Then he left.

For goodness' sake, that was it now. I had seriously had enough! The management showed all new members around the club, so I guessed he hadn't liked what he had seen, and now gone. Oh well, you win some, you lose some. I took small sips of my drink just in case anyone else came into the bar area. I might as well keep my options open, and my legs closed, until then. I drank my drink and was about to leave when he suddenly reappeared. I was definitely staying now!

He went to the bar, and I saw cash change hands, so he had obviously now joined as a new member of the club. This had better be fucking good, I was thinking to myself, staring at him. He bought a drink and looked at me – the only sad, lonely person in the bar area. The other couple had finished playing pool and were talking in another quiet corner. I looked at him, smiled and said, 'For goodness' sake, please sit down near me for a minute, as I feel like a right Billy no-mates,' and laughed. He looked at me and also grinned. I told him it wasn't a come-on but that I felt a bit of an idiot, sat by myself, and I was just about to leave as I was bored.

We talked and introduced ourselves, which sounded a bit formal but what the heck. He said he was called Lee and had driven from near Sheffield for a night out in Hull. I said as much as I loved Hull, I could think of better places to come for a night out. We laughed about my still-prevalent Hull accent, even though I didn't live in Hull anymore. I couldn't tell if he thought it was my accent, or me, that was funny, but who cared? I didn't, as I was now certainly ready for some fun.

He explained that he had left the club to find a cashpoint to withdraw some cash as they wouldn't accept card payments at the club. Then came back to join as a member. After all, he had driven all this way. He wasn't going to just head back home again – yet. I said I understood and guessed the reason he had come to Hull was because he didn't want anyone to recognise him. Lee agreed, said he was married with young children, but his wife and children were away visiting family this bank holiday weekend. He had to work, so was at home – alone.

He had decided to make the most of it, by going out. I told him, laughing, 'You are so fucking naughty!' with a twinkle in my eye. I wasn't letting him go easily. He brazenly admitted he had been to clubs before, and even said he loved his wife, but things were missing. 'What? Like blow jobs and sex?' I added quickly, now biting my lip like I was a character in *Fifty Shades of Grey*. I had definitely been on those chatlines far too long, and sexual words now flowed freely out of my mouth without any embarrassment. Worryingly, I had no verbal or sexual filter anymore.

'Yeah,' Lee replied in agreement.

This was the usual story from married men, or men that were in a 'relationship': their partner didn't have time for sex and was too tired at the end of the day after looking after the children. I seriously understood it; I would be tired too. I had been there, done that, many years previously, got divorced, remarried, now widowed, and could do whatever I wanted to do, with whomever I wanted to. People may judge me, but that's not my problem. Look at it this way – Lee went into a swingers' club, looking for sex. If it wasn't with me, it would be with someone else. I certainly wasn't responsible for these men being unfaithful.

Lee finished his drink. I couldn't be bothered anymore with small talk, or his guilty feelings; after all, we were both in the club for one reason only. Let's just say that five minutes later we were in a private room upstairs in that swingers' club, having good intensive sex. The other couple that were in the bar had already left. There were only us two alone in the club. We were both loud and noisy in that locked room. It was naughty and almost forbidden, but I didn't care. I could do what the hell I wanted – and I did.

We got dressed and left the club, both with no regrets. I gave him my mobile number. The next day, he made contact. After all, his wife and children were still away from home. He was at work but would be finishing late afternoon. We arranged for him to visit me at my house, as it was nearer than travelling into Hull. Sometimes, you just had to be practical and save on fuel costs! Thinking of saving the planet and all that! We had a continuation of the previous night, but in more private surroundings.

A few hours later, Lee said he had better go home to do some housework as his wife would have expected him to do some whilst she was away. I understood. It was like a secret life, a fix. Something to break the monotony of the commitment, and ties, of a marriage or relationship. To make life worth living, to put a smile on his face. Life is too short. I think in the future I should rename bank holidays as wank holidays. It just seems more appropriate. Here's to the next swinging wank holiday!

CHAPTER 21

SUICIDE BLONDE

'I have one massive regret in my life – that I was still working HERE when my husband was fucking dying.'

Those words are what I almost spat out to my ex-employer at my exit interview. It was said with hatred, spite and venom, and I meant it. Every bloody word of it. I even shocked myself by saying it with such ferocity.

I was fucking done with it all. Pathetic working policies, meaningless statistics, absurd appraisals, verbal warnings – I was done with it all! Bloody big time!

Did they think I enjoyed the relentless, mundane, manic helpdesk? I was like a robot, or someone on autopilot. Every time the phone rang, my heart would skip a beat with the stress of knowing that all the telephone calls were recorded and monitored. My blood pressure was high and I felt ill from the stress of work. One slip-up and I would be pulled up on it, as I had been before. I was bloody done with this. I wasn't a child. Although I felt I had almost regressed into one, as if I was still at home as a young child, frightened, with Mother watching my every move, stifling me and berating me for everything I did under her constant watch.

I knew I was worth more than this. They were so full of control, conflict and contradictions. I didn't even want to get into an argument about it. I was done. I had been pushed too far this time. It was all false to me now; the false nails, false eyelashes, false boobs, false sympathy, false teeth even – I just didn't fucking care anymore. It was all false. I restrained myself from becoming angry. I was so fucking done with it, more than they would ever know. I hated and despised working.

I couldn't even shout or act angrily, as I had been too poorly over the last few months with tonsillitis and glandular fever, and my throat was still sore. I now, unusually, spoke with a quiet, husky, toned voice. I was tired with stress and exhaustion. I finally had a nervous breakdown.

I certainly didn't need this shit. I had enough shit on my plate; in fact, more shit than anyone else would even be able to deal with in their lifetime. I needed time out. Time to reflect on Andrew's death, his mother's death, my life-threatening tumour that had now left my body physically scarred, my mother's death and my mental health. The whole lot was too overwhelming and exhausting to even think about anymore.

I walked away. Away from the treadmill and the pressure cooker of work. Out of a secure job and into the lion's den of the unknown. I seriously didn't care anymore. I needed calm not conflict, and time to reflect on my way forward in life. For the first time ever in the whole of my life, I needed 'me time'.

I remembered the words of Dannii ... *Always walk away if you feel uncomfortable and NEVER EVER do anything you don't want to do.*

Well, I DIDN'T want to do it anymore, and I WOULDN'T do it anymore. I felt like I had been a bird in a cage that had suddenly been released. I flew – away from it all.

There was only me to look out for, and if it all went wrong, it would be my own fault. I could live with that. I would make my own way in life, with or without a job, with or without money, with or without men. I took a step back and evaluated my private life. It HAD to change. Gone are the one-night stands and swingers' clubs. My curiosity had been satisfied. I now needed to be grounded again and realistic with my future plans.

Life is getting better again, and I am free. I am my own person, ready to explore challenges, have adventures and open doors – or even kick them open if necessary, to a new, different life. I cannot turn the clock back to erase and rewind. I have to move forward, slowly.

I know I am a suicide blonde, in many ways, and have an unknown future. But I am strong, a survivor, and ready to embrace life. Life really is too short, as I know only too well.

Andrew will always be in my heart and around me, loved and never forgotten. XXXXX

www.ingramcontent.com/pod-product-compliance
Lightning Source LLC
LaVergne TN
LVHW041624070426
835507LV00008B/445